D1051550

Catalog-in-Publication Data

O'Brien, Patrick S.

Making College Count: A Real World Look at How to
Succeed In and After College / Patrick O'Brien. – 2nd ed.

250 p. : ill. ; 20.9 cm.

ISBN 978-0-615-39440-4 (pbk.)

I. College student orientation - United States 2. College
students - United States - Psychology 3. Success I. Title

Library of Congress Control Number 2010912070

Published by Patrick O'Brien Enterprises, LLC
Cincinnati, Ohio
www.MakingCollegeCountBook.com

**For bulk book purchases, e-mail
Books@MakingCollegeCountBook.com.**

Printed in the United States of America

Making
COLLEGE COUNT

EDITION 2

Patrick S. O'Brien

First Edition

First Print .... November 1996

Second Print .... April 1997

Third Print .... April 1998

Fourth Print .... July 1999

Fifth Print .... April 2000

Sixth Print .... July 2001

Seventh Print .... October 2002

Eighth Print .... May 2003

Ninth Print .... September 2005

Tenth Print .... May 2008

Eleventh Print .... March 2009

Second Edition

First Print .... August 2010

Illustrations by Pete Adams
Design by Jennifer Greiner

MakingCollegeCountBook.com

TABLE OF CONTENTS

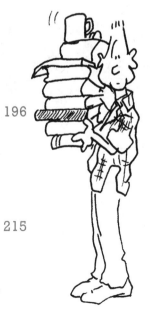

NECESSARY THANKS

Thanks to the literally thousands of business and professional leaders, high school and college educators, job interviewees, parents, students, Making It Count staffers and speakers, and friends whose thoughts and ideas have helped shape this book.

Since co-founding Making It Count in 1998, I have met, been influenced by, and been inspired by literally thousands of high school and college educators. There are far too many to thank individually. However, I'd be remiss if I didn't say thank you to all those dedicated counselors, teachers, professors, administrators, and school staff members who have guided and advised me through the years.

From this group of amazing individuals, Making It Count developed a National Educator Advisory Board. These professionals give the Making It Count organization countless hours of time to provide their insights on relevant trends in education and what's working for students in their schools.

I'd be remiss if I didn't say **thank you** to all those dedicated **counselors**, **teachers**, **professors**, **administrators**, and **school staff members** who have guided and advised me through the years.

Making It Count has also developed a National Student Advisory Council. Its purpose is to help keep the organization current with students across the nation.

Thanks also to the 250 or so people who survived the interview process and have actually had to work for me over the past 20 years. Each of them has added to the thoughts and ideas in "Making College Count."

Special thanks go to three close friends, Brad Baker, Marilyn Muldowney (now Marilyn O'Brien), and Barb Miller. With tremendously successful careers after earning degrees from Harvard University, Ithaca College, and Vanderbilt University respectively, they have added greatly to the book.

After the original publication of this book, Brad Baker and I co-founded Making It Count. Brad, in a range of roles including president of the company, was a major driving force in growing

Making It Count. He's a brilliant guy who has had a tremendous impact on the organization over the past 10 years.

J.R. Cifani has also played a very special role in Making It Count. After starting in 1998 as one of the first 13 speakers, he has, over the past decade, become the leader of the organization. Without him, and the support of the parent company Monster Worldwide, there would be no Making It Count company and no updated "Making College Count." His leadership has been foundational and pivotal.

I also want to thank, in advance, the many people who will call or write to offer their assistance as "much needed" editors for this book. Let me respond up front by saying that the book is meant to "talk" to you. To accomplish this required taking a few liberties with the rules of grammar. I do know "proper" English. I just didn't want it to get in the way of our "conversation."

SO WHO IS THIS GUY?

Where do I start?

Writing about how to approach college to build your successful future is much easier than writing about myself. But, to lend credibility to the chapters that follow, I think it's important to share with you a bit about my background.

My name is Pat O'Brien. Prior to going to college, I was pretty much focused on having fun and getting through high school with a minimal amount of effort. My idea of hitting the books was skimming my notes in study hall and homeroom. Playing football, working, working out, and driving my 12-year-old Mustang were the extent of my extracurricular activities.

My grades in high school were decent, a bit above a 3.0. I

thought I was doing just fine, doing what I needed to in order to stay ahead of the pack. My older brother and sister had attended Notre Dame. I assumed I'd be heading there as well until Notre Dame very politely informed me that they didn't think I was a "fit." It was a bit of a wake-up call, but one I brushed off as I liked the idea of going in a different direction than my older siblings. I *was* accepted at Miami University (in Ohio) as well as Ohio State and San Diego State and decided to head to Miami to get out on my own, have a great time, and get a college degree in the process.

Leading up to my high school graduation, I was mentally gearing up for a summer of working 60 to 70 hours per week pulling weeds for Sandy's Landscaping to help pay for my education. My parents would also help with my college expenses, and I planned to take on student loan debt to pay the rest. I was more than willing to do this, though, because I *knew* that I'd get a great job after I got my degree.

I was a man with a plan—at least I thought I was—until my high school senior class awards assembly. The assembly was the type of event that I would typically sleep through, but I left it feeling like I'd been hit in the stomach with a baseball bat.

At the event, fellow classmates were honored for scholarships they had received. I was literally blown away at the hundreds of thousands of dollars in awards being announced — not just for

athletics, but for "outstanding academic achievement."
A lot of kids got free money. I was shocked.

What did I get? Nothing — nothing but a sick feeling thinking that I'd be pulling weeds for 10 hours every day and going into big debt to go to college while many of my classmates would be going for free or at a significantly reduced cost. It was a painfully clear statement that I was not *leading* the pack; I was well back in it. My "efforts" hadn't gotten me where I wanted to be.

Two thoughts raced through my head. The first was that this whole situation was terribly unfair. These people weren't brilliant. I had known many since grade school and they were certainly no brain surgeons! I was a pretty smart guy. I should have been getting *some* of this "free money," shouldn't I?

The second thought — which was even more disturbing — was that these same people, and people like them, would be getting the best jobs — the jobs that *I* wanted —after college if I didn't somehow get to the front of the pack.

I decided that day to do whatever it took in college to be first in line for a great job when I graduated. I became committed to success — right there in that high school assembly. It sounds a little dramatic, but it was an important day in my life.

It would still be a couple of years before I had a true understanding of the keys to being first in line. While I was figuring it out, I made some educated guesses and substituted hard work for my lack of full understanding. I constantly searched for the answers — observing the habits of successful students and talking to countless professors and professionals. In the process, I learned what I needed to know to make college count.

After four extremely enjoyable years of college, I started my career at Procter & Gamble in Brand Management/Marketing. It was a highly sought-after role — one of the best opportunities available for a college graduate. More than half of the people hired for the role were MBA's from *top schools*. Many more were undergrads from Ivy League schools — and there I was, stepping into the role with my undergraduate degree from an Ohio public school.

The best thing about the experience may have been that I didn't even actively pursue the job. *Based on my resume*, P&G came after me. Based on my strong college record, I was (at least on paper) the type of candidate they wanted for the job.

Another point worth mentioning is that I interviewed for five jobs and received four offers from well-respected companies. Two offers were in accounting, one in finance, and one in brand management. Said another way, the principles in this book can open doors — good doors — even if you're not yet sure which doors you want opened.

After graduation, I got off to a fast start at P&G, and within three years I became a brand manager, helping to run the $400,000,000 Crest toothpaste business. I worked hard to achieve this, but I never would have had the opportunity to do so if I hadn't had the record in college that got me the interview.

At Procter & Gamble, I also had the opportunity to begin interviewing college students for brand management roles. After extensive training, I was out talking to college seniors who wanted to work for this great company.

After interviewing a significant number of job candidates, my thoughts on what made up the perfect candidate crystallized. Only after I had become a "recruiter" of college students did I realize how critical great choices are *throughout* college for success in the job search process.

At age 27, I left Procter & Gamble to become the Director of Marketing for The Branigar Organization, a developer of private golf communities in the southeastern United States. I lived in and nationally marketed The Landings on Skidaway Island, a gated island community off the coast of Savannah. If you've never lived on a private island, it's a pretty nice life. I'd highly recommend it.

At age 30, I was promoted to Vice President/General Manager at Champion Hills, a spectacular new community in the mountains of North Carolina. In the role, I managed a $20,000,000 real estate development and a staff of 90 employees. I interviewed, hired, and managed people in a wide range of occupations. But regardless of whether it was an executive chef, security chief, construction manager, horticulturist, or financial controller, I always looked to see if the candidates exhibited a set of **Winning Characteristics** before I hired them. I'll explain the **Winning Characteristics** later in the book.

Many of the ideas in "Making College Count" came from these experiences. The actual idea for "Making College Count" came out of a conversation I had with my younger sister as she was heading off to college. As mentioned, I learned how to be successful in college by talking to a lot of successful people, via trial and error, and by stumbling through various good and bad decisions. I thought that I could give my sister a huge advantage if I could give her the understanding of how to approach college as a freshman that most students don't figure out until junior or senior year.

The notes from that conversation sat in my desk drawer for years, but as I learned more and more about college recruiting and interviewed more and more candidates for different kinds of jobs during my own career, the idea of "Making College Count" went from being an idea that I might pursue "someday" to something of great interest to me.

Adding fuel to the fire, in conversations with Brad Baker, I learned what the companies he had recruited for were looking for in job candidates. As you can probably guess, what they were looking for was remarkably similar to what I had experienced with my employers. They too were looking for the **Winning Characteristics**. After many discussions, we got very excited about the idea of teaching students how to *create* a college experience where they actually built the **Winning Characteristics** and could *prove* to employers on interview day that they owned these skills.

So, at 33, Brad and I left corporate America to grow "Making College Count" into a dynamic learning program to give students a road map to success. We called the company Making It Count and focused on delivering live, in-school, success presentations to students. Thirteen years later, the company has delivered programs to more than 23,000,000 students in schools across the nation. It has more than 200 amazing speakers giving a total of eight different Making It Count programs, with a dedicated staff of more than 30 people helping manage more than 10,000 speaking engagements Making It Count schedules each year.

Making It Count is now a part of Monster Worldwide. Monster is the world's most trusted job search resource — so the Making It Count organization has learned a great deal from being a part of the Monster family. It's been a great opportunity to get an even closer look at employers and what they are looking for in job candidates.

One other element of my career worth mentioning is that since originally writing "Making College Count," I have become a college adjunct professor. Working with another good friend, Donn Davis (one of the original architects of the AOL success story), we created a class called Real Strategies for Real Business. The goal was to teach the class to 25 top business students at Miami University for one year as a way to give back to the school. Roger Jenkins, the progressive Dean of the Farmer School of Business at Miami, took a chance on us and let us teach our innovative class. Eight years later, we're still teaching. It's been a real life "learning lab" for "Making College Count."

In developing relationships with the students who took our class, I think we've *learned* as much as we've *taught* over eight years. The experience has greatly evolved my perspective on college success and played a major role in shaping this new and improved edition of "Making College Count." Special thanks to former students Chris Mack for his thoughtful input on the book and Mackenzie Bruce for her helpful editing.

The writing (and rewriting) of "Making College Count" has been a part of a career path that has been rewarding for me. You may define your goals very differently. That's perfectly fine. What's key is creating the opportunity to achieve *YOUR* vision of success.

What has worked for me? A *lot* of work, good decision making, and a little luck. One thing I'm certain of, though, is that it was the principles in this book that put me in that great first job and gave me the chance to show what I could do.

While there are no guarantees in life (or in this book), with your commitment, the ideas that follow will help you maximize your opportunities and reach your personal goals.

CHAPTER 1

The Rules of the Game

Before you do *anything*, if you plan to do it well, you learn how success is defined, how difficult it is to achieve it, and what the rules of the "game" are. It only makes sense.

Your college experience should be no different.

The following three chapters will help you understand how the "judges," your *potential* future employers (and top grad schools), define college success. More specifically, these chapters will help you understand how recruiters view the hiring process and how they choose which students get the *BEST* opportunities after graduation.

Unfortunately, the following chapters will also give you a few statistics on how well today's students are doing. They aren't pretty.

Students are crashin' and burnin' out there.

So here's the critical point: Understanding all this *now*, as opposed to *after* your senior year, will help you make *much* better decisions during your days at college. That's the key!

If you understand how the judges define success, what your odds are of achieving it, and how the rules have been set for the game, you're more likely to achieve success than if you don't understand these things. Said another way, you'll score a lot more touchdowns in football if you understand what a goal line is, where it's located on the field, and the rules involved in getting the ball over that line. It's really very simple and quite logical.

One more important point. There's no *one* right way to be successful in (or after) college. Every individual defines success differently and there are many ways to achieve success *if* you understand the process.

> There is **no one right way** to be successful in (or after) college.

You'll be introduced to a broad range of concepts in this book. *All* of them won't be right for you. But, they are proven approaches to success. They do work. As such, they'll give you a strong framework for the process. Many are timeless. Based on current trends on campus and in college recruiting, many others have been updated for this new edition of the book. Your personal interests, strengths, and common sense will guide you in how to make the concepts work for you (and give you insight as to when you need to take an alternate approach).

By the way, if you haven't read the "So Who is This Guy?" section, please take a quick look through it. Hopefully, it will reinforce the following: I've been there. I've done it. I can help you.

> So, if you want to be successful — listen up!

Why are You Going to College?

It's a good question and a good place to start.

Why are *YOU* going to college?

I don't want to know why your parents think you should go or why your friends are going. What matters is why *YOU* want to be there. This is really all about *YOUR* life — so their hopes and dreams for you are "nice," but once you hit campus, it's what's in *YOUR* head that really matters. Make sense?

Well-meaning "helicopter" parents who want to script every step of their student's entire life are very common these days. I think it's *GREAT* that yours care enough to spend the time mapping out your life. I like them even better if they bought you this book! *BUT*, they won't be standing next to you making the decision as to whether you choose to maximize your GPA or your social opportunities the night before a big test. They won't be helping you set priorities for finals week or studying for you at 10 p.m. on the Saturday night before finals (at least I hope they won't).

If you're shooting for the stars, read on.

You need to understand what college is all about for *you*, so well-meaning friends don't decide on your behalf that it's all about 24/7 partying. Make sense?

If you're going to college *just* for an "education" and aren't looking to start an amazing career as a result of it, let me save you some time. Don't read this book. It's not for you. On the other hand, if you'd like your college experience to be a launching process — elevating you to the most interesting, challenging, rewarding job you can get in your chosen field — you're in the right place.

Don't get me wrong. I think learning simply for the sake of learning is a worthwhile objective. Really, it is. In fact, I'll probably go back to school at some point for just that reason. You should *always* be in a learning mode. In a fast-paced, changing world, lifelong learning is a critical skill for everyone who wants to be successful. *However*, how you'll approach college on a day-to-day basis will be different depending upon how you define your college goals and set your priorities.

As a simple example, I will admit that the idea of entering a top MBA program to compete academically against some of the smartest rising stars in the world has always been intriguing to me. I like the idea of being able to say that I am a graduate of a top MBA program. However, it just wasn't a part of what I needed to do to get where I wanted to go in my career — so I never pursued it.

Let's look at a "real life" scenario that I faced as an undergrad that brings the issue to life. During my senior year, I had a choice between going to a class or a pre-interview reception thrown by Procter & Gamble. It was a class where the professor did *not* look kindly on people missing classes. However, the decision for me was a no-brainer. I went to the reception. It's simply a matter of priorities. I ask again… why are you going to college?

> If you're going to college to create your future by doing the things necessary to best position yourself for a successful, rewarding career, read on.

The Cold Hard Facts

Hang on. You're in for a rough chapter.

While *building* your future is your goal, it is important that you know that the campus landscape is littered with lost souls who are still looking for a hammer or a building site. Just to raise the stakes a bit, this is happening in an environment where the

The magnitude of the challenge can be overwhelming.

cost of higher education is skyrocketing. On the other hand, the difference in earnings between those who did and did not have a successful experience is large and growing. So, college is hard and more expensive but more important than ever.

Did I mention that it's tough out there?

Let's first look at the success statistics. As I mentioned, they're kind of ugly. Based on numbers released in 2009 by ACT:

- Only 68% of freshmen will return as sophomores (not very impressive)
- Among private schools, the number is only 70% (not much better)
- The two numbers above were 72% and 74%, respectively, 10 years ago (not a good trend)
- Only 26% will graduate in four years (this number is outdated… they no longer publish it)
- Only 49% will graduate in five years or less (they still publish this one)
- Only 40% seeking an associate degree will graduate in three years or less

Now let's lay a March 2009 National Center for Education Statistics number on top of that:

- Only six in 10 of those who do graduate will get a job that required a degree.

DO THE MATH. Only about three of 10 incoming freshmen seeking a four-year degree will graduate in five years or less *AND* get a job that required a degree. Not pretty.

And, the cost of failure is higher than ever. The average annual total cost (tuition, room and board, books, fees, etc.) for a student in 2009 was more than $18,000 for a public school and more than $37,000 for a private school (College Board, 2009). These annual costs have risen by approximately $10,000 each since this book was first published in 1996. Multiply that by four or five years and that's a lot of money to spend to get a job flipping burgers. Again, tough numbers.

Further complicating the issue, from an earnings standpoint, a college degree is now more important than ever. Based on U.S. Census Bureau statistics, a typical college graduate of a four-year college established in the workforce now makes almost double what a non-graduate makes. And, the spread between the two is growing dramatically.

Hangin' in there?

U.S. Average Annual Income

College Graduate	$59,016
High School Graduate	$32,304

And last but not least:

- More than 50% of college grads now return home to live with their parents

This number is based on a range of recent surveys of new college graduates. Some studies show the number as high as 80% in 2010!

On a lifetime earnings basis, according to statistics published by the U. S. Department of Labor (2007), a four-year college graduate will, on average, earn more than $1 million more in his/her lifetime than someone with only a high school diploma.

There are two ways to look at these statistics. The first is that the situation is *HOPELESS*. It's not. The other is that there is a *LOT* to be said for doing what is necessary in college to graduate, open doors, and build your successful future.

The pages that follow can help you beat the statistics.

Building Your Future

Three hours from now you're going to look at college *and your future* in a whole new way. You're going to look at it through the eyes of a recruiter, seeing opportunities (and pitfalls) that you didn't even know existed.

You'll think differently about what's important to do in and out of the classroom, and have insights that *other* students may not have for many years. You'll watch many fall by the wayside or graduate into jobs they could have gotten without a college degree. You'll know college is about more than showing up and trying to get decent grades. You'll think of college as an opportunity to build a successful future.

Along with getting a degree, the objective of college, in my opinion, is to build a track record *loaded* with the qualities

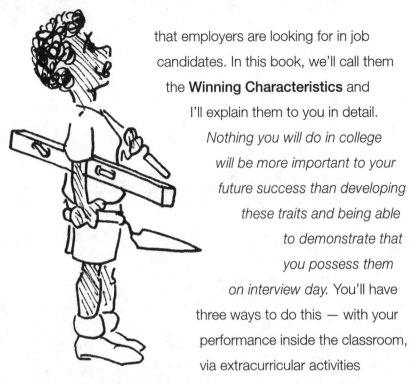

that employers are looking for in job candidates. In this book, we'll call them the **Winning Characteristics** and I'll explain them to you in detail. *Nothing you will do in college will be more important to your future success than developing these traits and being able to demonstrate that you possess them on interview day.* You'll have three ways to do this — with your performance inside the classroom, via extracurricular activities outside the classroom (including volunteer work), and through meaningful work experience. Each of these offers tremendous opportunities to develop, sharpen, and clearly exhibit the **Winning Characteristics**.

To be successful, you'll need to take care of some basics. Along with picking a school and a major, you'll need to master a few critical skills that will allow you to take on the complex challenges that you will face during your college experience. *This book will help you do that.*

Then, with the basics in your grasp, your academics, extracurricular activities, and employment experiences will provide golden opportunities to develop and impressively exhibit the **Winning Characteristics**. Each will be a part of the foundation upon which you'll build your successful future.

Discover a proven, solid structure
for success, one that will allow you
to be whatever you want to be.

CHAPTER 2
If You're Not There Yet

If you're already in college or have picked your school and major with a high degree of confidence, you can just skim the next two sections. You've already been through the thought process (I hope) that will be shared in these sections. If not, read on.

I'll start with some "simple" questions. What do you want to do for the majority of your waking hours for the next 40 or so years? What fields can leverage your unique personality and skills and allow you to jump out of bed each day and feel good about what you'll be doing that day? Simply put, just what is it that's going to make you happy, help you reach your financial goals, and/or allow you to change the world?

> What do **you want to do** for the next 40 or so years?

A given interest can take you many different places.

Following from that, what schools could put you in the best position to interview for (and get) a great entry level position in that field — or in a field that you decide two years from now is a much better place for you to be?

These issues are among the most complex you've ever faced. And, the information you'll need to help you make the decisions may not seem readily available.

With an investment of your time, there is a tremendous amount of information available to assist you with the process.

And remember, nobody is going to *give* you the answers. To determine what is best for you, *you'll* need to take an active interest and lead the process. Let me repeat that. To determine what is best for you, *YOU'LL* need to take an active interest and lead the process. I know that in many cases, mom and dad will want to "help," and they should. But, the key word is *help*, not lead or "own" the process. They already picked their careers — and hopefully made great choices. Now it's time for *you* to plan *your* career.

> Remember, it's your life and
> your career. You own your future!

Choosing Your Major

I could write a whole book on this subject. In fact, others already have. High school and college counselors also have some pretty good tests to help you understand what fields might be a strong fit for your interests and talents. Let me share several thoughts about this critical area and see if I can help simplify the process for you.

First, pick something you fundamentally enjoy. It does not matter if you hear about a sales job where you could eventually earn up to a quarter of a million dollars a year. If you're not comfortable with people you don't know, are not outgoing by nature, and hate the idea of travel, odds are you won't be successful or happy in that role.

Second, pick something you think is a fit with your core

strengths as an individual — something you'll be good at. It will be difficult for you to be the next pop music sensation if you can't carry a tune. Grit and determination will take you a long way, but talent/ability/raw resource potential can make a difference too. Make sure you know your own skill set.

I would also recommend that you make the effort to talk to several professors in fields you're considering to understand the quantity and quality of jobs available in those fields. Most will have great perspectives. You can also look at a book published by the government called the "Occupational Outlook Handbook" (online version is at www.bls.gov/OCO.gov). You could never read the whole thing — it would be like reading the entire Wikipedia. That said, it will tell you a lot about any field of interest, including what people in the field do every day, what the starting salaries are, what salary progression in that field typically looks like, and what the job outlook for that field is in the future. A career placement office on any campus is also typically loaded with resources and information on the future potential for various career fields.

Pursue a passion with an eye on the job market.

Into which job fields will a particular major open doors? For instance, if you like mythology, it's much better to find out sooner rather than later that, unless you want to teach mythology, there are not a great number of jobs available that directly utilize this degree. That doesn't mean you'll be living in the streets — but you most likely will not be utilizing your knowledge of Zeus in your job.

Sometimes the best decision, at least for a little while, is no decision at all. Some schools will allow you to be an undeclared major. If you have no  idea what you want to do, this can be a legitimate way to delay a decision. It may allow you to take a wide range of classes your freshman year and get a taste of a variety of subjects (and do a full year of research) before making this call. Here is a *caveat*. If you want to go into a technical field — like engineering or architecture — and you want to graduate on schedule, it's better to start in those fields as a freshman than enter them later. These kinds of programs have very specific requirements, and it's usually *TOUGH* to graduate on time if you switch to these fields *during* college rather than starting in them from the outset.

So, before going in undeclared, clearly understand two things. First, will you still be able to graduate "on time?" And second, will you make it more difficult to get into high demand majors at your school by delaying your choice? Remember, every *extra* year you spend in college is a year you are likely driving yourself deeper into debt *and* not earning to your full potential.

Let's take the undeclared major concept to an extreme. An acquaintance of mine was in college for seven years, had *several* majors, but just didn't seem to be comfortable making a career choice — so he didn't. This is not a good thing. It's expensive and can eat up your life and empty your wallet!

After freshman year, make a call! If later on you think you made a mistake, change your major once. Get a degree. Get some real world experience. Then if you want to make a move, you'll have a solid experience base to build upon.

At this point, let me touch on another potentially dicey subject — choosing a major within liberal arts. There are some *good* and some *bad* reasons to do this. I'm not anti-liberal arts; I just want to get you to think about why you are choosing your path and what you plan to do with a degree in a particular field of study.

Let's start with some of the positives of a liberal arts education. Any student in a liberal arts major will receive a well rounded education. The individual should, through his studies, learn how to think at a complex level, write well, communicate effectively, and develop and sharpen his problem-solving skills. This type of personal growth, by the way, should result from any successful college education (and can be built upon with a quality internship if you can secure one). And, any liberal arts major will have the opportunity to prove to his future employer that he possesses the **Winning Characteristics** (more on that later) *if* he can get an interview for the job he wants. Just like any major, achievements and activities outside the classroom can be huge assets to a liberal arts major.

A strong performance in liberal arts might be viewed positively by a large company hiring for a non-technical job (not accounting, engineering, finance, IT, etc), an organization in that specific field of study, or a graduate school — all potentially great places to be.

The concern with some fields of study within liberal arts is their day-to-day applicability in the "real world." Some like English and math have strong merit here. But if after graduation you want to go to work for a small to mid-sized organization, go to work in a more technical field, or even start your own company, studying French literature or philosophy *might* not get you where you want to go.

Here's the distinction. Large firms and graduate schools plan to teach you the specific skills you'll need for future employment. When I interviewed for my job at Procter & Gamble, the recruiters told me that they didn't care about my lack of marketing course work. The company knew more about marketing than most colleges and would teach me what I needed to know after I got the job. Obviously, in this case, a liberal arts major would have been fine.

Now let's look at the other side of the coin. Most of the job growth in the future is projected to come from small companies. Small companies (fewer than 500 employees) now employ more than half of the workforce and create 60-80% of the new jobs in this country (Source: SBA Office of Advocacy). Given that, you're *very* likely to go to work for a small company — or perhaps even start one.

Many small organizations cannot afford the comprehensive training programs that big companies have historically offered. They will, therefore, be more interested in hiring someone who has an education that is more specifically related to and more relevant to the particular position they are trying to fill.

Finally, a liberal arts major should *not* be used as a vehicle to allow you to avoid making a decision as to what you want to do after college to "keep your options open." As I've just explained, a liberal arts education will open some doors but it will close others. You *will* be making decisions about your future by taking this route. So make your decisions wisely.

Getting back to the general subject, picking a major can be difficult and nerve-racking. How can you decide what you want to do before you ever do it? What if you make the wrong choice?

After you pick a major and have moved into the stage of second guessing yourself (almost everyone does), here are three things to think about.

First, everyone else is just as confused as you are. If they aren't *today*, they most likely will be at some point in the next four years!

Second, internships will shed some light on the issue. They will give you a much better understanding of the type of work you would actually be doing in a particular field. I'll talk more about internships later.

Third, do not feel limited by your major. You can interview for and get a job outside of your major if you follow the principles in "Making College Count." As mentioned earlier, you probably can't become a mechanical engineer without a technical degree, but you will have non-technical options available to you. I did.

In my case, I had a double major of finance and accounting. After an accounting internship at a bank, I had serious doubts as to whether or not this was what I wanted to do with the rest of my life. It was a good job. It was a good company. It just wasn't what I wanted to do every day for the next 40 years — okay, not even for one year.

I did not change my major as I was committed to graduating in four years. The fact that I was out of money helped "encourage" me to meet this commitment and graduate on time. So, I

interviewed not only for finance and accounting jobs, but for marketing and sales positions as well. As you know (if you read the "So Who is This Guy" section), I was offered and took a job in brand management/marketing.

Another point worth making is that you are not bound for life to your major even if you take your first job in that field. Many people move from one department to another in an organization after they find that they like something better than the field they originally chose. In fact, having a couple of different departmental perspectives (and relationships within two groups) can be a real advantage to an employee working in a team setting. In some cases, breadth of experience can also help you move up more quickly in management. The more experiences you have, the more options you will have if you want to switch companies or if your current employer downsizes.

By the way, with the marketplace changing as fast as it is, the odds are you won't take only one job and retire from it anyway. The statistics change every year, but most sources estimate that students graduating today will have as many as 15 or more jobs with 10 or more companies during their careers. Even if you are one of the *rare* few who will stay with one company for the next 40 years, you will most likely play a variety of roles for that organization during your career.

So, choosing a major is important. But contrary to popular belief, you're not making a decision that you'll have to live with for the rest of your life.

Picking Your School

Start with the finish line in your sight.

You want to get a great job coming out of college. Pick schools that are best positioned to help you do this. The social element of college is also important and shouldn't be overlooked. *However*, picking a school just because it's in a fun city, has a top 10 football team, or has a reputation for great parties is probably not a brilliant move.

Take a broad approach to your college search. Also remember, there are many options for school now: traditional public and private four-year programs, two-year programs, 2+2 programs, as well as colleges offering courses or degrees online. It's all about researching your options and choosing what is best for you. By the way, even if you can afford a private school, also consider public school opportunities. A public school *may* be outstanding in your particular field of interest. It *might* be a much better value than a particular private school. *Make sure you check out all the higher education opportunities available to you.*

Regardless of the school you choose, you can make great friends and have a *LOT* of fun at any school you pick, so make your decision based on career-driven factors, not social ones. Let me give you more perspective on how to do that.

If you have some feel as to what area of study you want to go into (natural science, architecture, business, health care, etc.), find out which schools have a strong reputation in that field. There are a number of publications and companies that rank colleges. There are also resources that evaluate online degree granting schools. Each ranking system is based on different factors. None truly gives the whole picture. However, if you look at a range of them, they can offer you some helpful direction.

A counselor can also be a big help in creating an initial list of colleges of interest. On the subject of counselors, if you're already utilizing them, keep doing so. If you aren't, you'll need to get over your fear of "adults" trying to offer "guidance." Most counselors have a great deal of meaningful information and perspective to share that can serve you well as you look for colleges that match your goals.

Along with counselors and college career center staff, talk to anyone you know who is in a career field that interests you. They will have some real world insight on which colleges prepare students well for success in a given field.

WESTERN STATE U. TECH POLY

You can go online to develop an initial list of colleges of interest. Look at sites like act.org, collegeboard.org, admissions.com, mycollegeoptions.org, collegebound.net, petersons.com, collegeview.com, knowhow2go.com, etc. There are a lot of college search tools out there. Try several (as they don't all use similar criteria) and see which colleges match up to criteria of interest to you.

One key thing to mention here is that if you are uncertain about your major, you'll want to choose a school that is not too specialized, one that will give you many different options if you decide to change your major. Going to a specialized nursing school is not a brilliant idea if you're not sure you want to be a nurse.

If you really don't know what you want to do, find out what a school you are considering will do to help undeclared majors find a good major for them. Related to that, find out how difficult it is at a given school to change your major. Some schools make it easy. Others make it extremely difficult. It might surprise you, by the way, that many students change their majors at least once.

During your junior year in high school (or earlier), you should begin writing, e-mailing and/or visiting schools you are considering to learn more about them. Many schools will send you information on their own, possibly adding to the list of options you actively pursue. Make sure you check out college websites. Go to college fairs. Visit with admissions officers who come to your high school.

After exploring a range of options online and digging through the college marketing material (brochures) sent to you, you'll need to narrow your options. Discard material from schools that are unappealing to you. Try to find friends or older brothers and sisters of friends who are attending schools of interest to you to get their perspectives. Get on the Internet to see what has been written on the schools in blogs, websites, magazines and newspapers. Don't believe *everything* you read. A junior at a school who just flunked a test who is ranting on her blog may not be objective at that moment. However, tons of information exists — use what is there to make the best decisions possible for you.

There are many good college guidebooks available, but I think you can learn a lot more a lot faster on the Web. And yes, this process requires a little work, but you'll be amazed by how much you'll learn. It's all about efficiently getting the information to help you make the best decisions for *YOU*.

Visit the schools you are considering. Talk to some of the students who are enrolled there. Sit in on a class or two to get a feel for the place and talk with professors. And, back to our objective of setting yourself up for a great job, spend some time at the colleges' career planning and placement offices. Find out who interviews on campus and get any data the offices may have on the success their past graduates have had in getting into grad school or getting jobs before and after graduation. Find out why they think their students do well in landing great jobs. Don't be shy. This is a big decision. Remember, your future is riding on it. No pressure, though.

If you can't visit, there are ways to conduct a virtual visit via the web. There are a range of virtual tours offered and colleges have more information available via their websites than ever before. That said, if at all possible, visit a school in person before making a commitment to attend.

Your high school counselor can help get you moving in the right direction. She will probably have a lot of students she needs to help so she won't have time to "own" the process for you. She can give you *direction* as *YOU* navigate the process. Get as much help/guidance from your counselor as you can. The better

SCHOOL INFO

she gets to know you, by the way, the more helpful she'll be able to be as this is a very personal process.

There is also now an entire college admissions industry. Lots of people will be willing to "help" you — for a fee, of course. Remember, you can get good information and make great decisions without spending a fortune.

Also, it is a good idea to apply to a range of schools, and probably three or four at a minimum. I would suggest a "vertical" list of schools. Look at the typical level of achievement of students that a school accepts as well as what percentage of the applicants are accepted at the school. Also apply to a range of schools in terms of difficulty of admission—matching your statistics to the admissions data of the schools. It's okay to have a *dream* school on the list, but make sure you remember the word "vertical" as you build your list.

Even if you are a high achiever, applying only to Harvard, Princeton, and Dartmouth would not be a successful use of the vertical list strategy. And, of course, a top school is a school that is well respected in your field of interest. If you're interested in accounting, the top schools are different than the top schools for journalism or education. Many people do change majors, so a school with strong programs in a number of areas of interest to you may be a great choice. Finally, if you don't think you can afford a given school but still think you're a great fit for it, apply! If you're a strong candidate, the school may be able to provide more financial aid than you had anticipated.

Here's an important caveat: There should be at least one school on your list you're reasonably sure will admit you and that you'd be happy to attend if that's where you end up. Applying only to schools that have average freshman SAT scores that are 200 points above yours may lead to great stress in the spring of your senior year and not only severely limit your options, but also could leave you shut out of a place to begin college.

It happens.

By the way, applying to schools "just to see" if you can get in if you have no plans to attend is a waste of money and just adds to the millions and millions of applications that must be evaluated each year. Save yourself the money. And, save the admissions office the unnecessary work and don't apply.

Let me mention the importance of timing. If a school you are considering has *rolling admissions* — meaning that they accept qualified students as applications are completed, get your application in early. When the class is filled, even highly qualified applicants may be shut out. There are many strategies you can use related to "early decision" and "early action" policies at schools. Admissions policies have become very complicated. Talk with your high school counselor and check out nacacnet. org to see all the types of admissions options that schools may now offer.

A couple of other points worth covering...

First, if you think as a college student you'll want or need a lot of personal attention, you may want to strongly consider a small school or a small program within a big school. If you want to be able to ask questions freely or spend quality time one-on-one with your professors, this may be more easily accomplished at a small school or in a small program at a big school.

On the other hand, if you don't think you will require a lot of personal time or attention, a big program or a larger school can be an excellent option. Larger schools or programs will sometimes have recognized leaders in a field as professors while smaller schools may not. Said another way, a world-renowned scientist may be more likely to teach at a large or prestigious school than at a small regional college.

Second, take the application process seriously. Spend a good amount of time on your application to make sure that you're presenting yourself as well as you can. The upcoming section on the **Winning Characteristics** will give you a feel for the types of things a college may be looking for in an applicant. If you're in doubt, your counselors and college admissions officers can be helpful here, as well.

Unless the school conducts interviews (some more competitive ones do), your application will be your only opportunity to show your stuff. Spell check and grammar check aren't enough. If you talked in your essay about how excited you are to be a part of a university's School of Bunnies (instead of School of Business), a spell check will not save you. You need to actually check and edit your work the old-fashioned way. Definitely have someone proof your essays, but remember they need to be *your* work. It is *your* voice that the admissions office wants to hear. And, you don't want to appear to be careless or not genuinely interested. It does make a difference.

Third, if you think you'll want to study abroad for a semester or a year, research the subject as a part of your decision-making process. Interest in this has increased as we have moved toward a global economy, and some schools are better set up than others to offer opportunities in this area. As a part of this, find out if financial aid/scholarships that you may receive apply to travel abroad programs.

Fourth, after you've been at college for a month, plan on feeling as if you picked the wrong school. You'll probably miss your family and friends and be sick of dining hall food, residence hall living, and/or laundry. Wait at least three months to decide if you've chosen the right school. You'll most likely "settle in" and like it more after you get a bit more comfortable and make a few more friends.

And last, but not least, take some comfort in the fact that *WHAT YOU ACCOMPLISH* while you're in college is probably more important than the school at which you accomplish it. Go to the best school you are admitted to (and can afford) but know that fewer than 2% of students go to Ivy League schools and that the world is full of highly successful people from colleges of all types.

> You can be highly successful coming out of any school.

CHAPTER 3
The Winning Characteristics

"*THIS* is the job. The right organization. The right people. The right work. And, the right salary. I have got to get this job!"

"Now, how in the world am I going to get it?"

All too often, this is a thought pondered for the first time by college seniors who are beginning their job search process and thinking about the *BIG* interview coming up next week.

It will take years to develop them, not a few weeks or months.

"What is the magic answer that will separate me from the other 15 students the recruiter will talk to that day?" What's the best response to that dreaded question, "What would your friends say is your biggest weakness?"

*It takes more than
a great suit
to get a great job.*

So, what's *THE* key to success in the interview process? Is it the proper shine on your shoes? Is it a conservative suit or a well-starched white shirt or blouse? Or is it whether your resume is typed in the right font or printed on white or tan paper?

Unfortunately, for all but a few of the individuals asking these questions, they've already missed the boat. They have already completely given up the chance to do the things that will truly set them apart from and put them above the crowd.

The things these students are contemplating have very little impact on the recruiter's decision-making process. He or she couldn't care less whether you spent $200 or $600 on your interview suit or whether your tie is striped or patterned (as long as you are clean and presentable)!

No matter what job you're pursuing, your employer will be looking for a well-rounded individual with strengths in several key areas. It takes *years* of focus on them, not a few weeks or months, to be able to develop them and prove to a recruiter that you possess them. They are the pillars that future success will be built upon. They are **Winning Characteristics** — and they are the difference between *success* and *failure* in the interview process.

Career Commonalities

You may question whether or not the **Winning Characteristics** apply to you. You may be interested in a new job in a new field that didn't even exist five years ago. How could they apply?

Well, they do.

When you boil it down, whether you are in a new or old field, whether you are a computer software designer, an engineer, a physical therapist, or an accountant, you have the same job. Your goal (and responsibility) is to solve problems and satisfy customers... with customers being anyone who pays to utilize your services or products. Think about it. There is no career where these two fundamental issues are not at the forefront of what you will do. Sure, the problems may present themselves in very different ways. They could be anything from a deteriorating bridge in need of stabilization to a puppy with a broken leg. Regardless of the specifics, you will be the person with the ability and desire to solve the problem, thereby satisfying your customer.

Your customers will come in all shapes and sizes, will potentially be located anywhere in the world, and may only interact with you by phone or online. They will be very diverse. In a way, even your boss and your fellow workers will be your customers. The correct way to define them is as internal customers. They work for the same organization as you do, but to be successful, and this might be a

surprise to you, you need to make them as happy as traditional customers outside of the company. If you make your external customers happy but drive your boss crazy, you'll soon be in need of a new job.

Even if you have zero interest in "business" or the thought of a "traditional" career path makes you cringe, you'll still be entering a job where you'll need to solve problems and/or satisfy customers.

Let's say, for instance, you'd like to spend your life teaching kindergarten to underprivileged youth. You'll still have a number of "customers" you'll need to satisfy. They include the principal, the superintendent of schools, and the school board. And, let's not forget the students or their very interested parents. In a sense, they're all customers. Hopefully, you'll help solve some of their problems and satisfy them in the process! So, as unique as different career choices may be, there are commonalities that make pursuing and succeeding in them remarkably similar.

Enter the **Winning Characteristics**.

As I mentioned in the "Building Your Future" section, they are the traits your future employer will be looking for — regardless of your chosen field. The **Winning Characteristics** will be the *key* to showing that you've got what it takes to solve problems and satisfy customers.

What Your Future Employer is Looking For

You will sink or swim based on the **Winning Characteristics**. They may be called different things in different fields. Some will call them "core competencies" and others have various catchy names for them, but, they are the pillars of success in *every* field! Key here is that I'm *not* talking about being able to look into the recruiter's eyes and say, "Yes, I have these skills." I'm talking about being able to give concrete examples of when and how you have exhibited them. You'll need to *prove* that you own them.

Here's why. A good bit of the interviewing you'll experience for high quality jobs will be what is called "behavioral-based" interviewing. The premise is actually quite simple. Most companies know what specific characteristics they are looking for in new hires. Their human resources staff will have spent a great deal of time and effort in determining which specific behavioral characteristics lead to success in the organization and perhaps in a specific job they are hiring for.

Behavioral-based interviewing will help recruiters determine which students have exhibited those characteristics in the past. They will ask you to "tell them about a time" when you showed the specific skills/traits they want in a new hire. They believe that if you have a proven track record of *exhibiting* leadership skills, for instance, that you're more likely to lead effectively in the future than someone who has not. It's a very logical approach. If you want someone who can communicate well, hiring someone who was on a debate team for four years is a safer bet than hiring someone from the chess team.

So, what are these critical **Winning Characteristics**?

I'll break them into seven key areas, built around the word COLLEGE.

- **C**ommunication Skills
- **O**rganizational Skills
- **L**eadership
- **L**ogic
- **E**ffort
- **G**roup Skills
- **E**ntrepreneurship

In the following pages, I'll describe each in detail. As an

incoming freshman, you may find this the most "distant," and therefore, most *BORING* part of the book. Regardless, I strongly encourage you to focus hard and really work to understand this section as it is the foundation for the entire book — and your successful future.

Communication Skills

To be effective, you have to be able to exchange information with other people. Pretty obvious, right? Concise, complete presentation of a situation, a problem, or a proposed solution in an organized manner is a fundamental skill that you'll need to master. The ability to effectively listen is equally challenging and important.

Given the fast pace of business today, oral communication skills are growing in importance relative to written skills. You will still need strong fundamental writing skills. That said, managers today just don't always have the luxury of having time to compose five-page documents to help make decisions.

Be aware that there is a difference between just "talking" and actually communicating. Communicating is not just about getting the message out—it's about someone else getting the message in. It involves someone actually *receiving* the message. You need to be able to deliver your thoughts in a way that is logical and well-organized so it actually makes an impact.

Taking the concept of communication one step further, let's go back to the fact that every employee of every kind has customers — someone whose problems you need to solve and/or you need to make happy, right? It might just be a boss or it could be someone who pays you money for a product or service. A key part of managing that relationship is highly effective communication with them.

To state the obvious, a strong grasp of computer skills is also an expectation. Additionally, the ability to e-mail (and speak) using "adult" language is an important skill. You need to sound like a professional, not a college kid trying to impress someone with the latest "text speak." That may seem very obvious, but I interact with many smart college seniors who both talk and e-mail with a great deal of slang and don't even know they're doing it.

Finally, many older adults in the workplace don't have a strong mastery of computer skills. Your expertise in this area and general comfort with technology are nice advantages (and an expectation on the part of any employer hiring a student graduating from college today).

Simply put, individuals who can communicate in a concise, well-organized fashion (both verbally and in writing) will be strongly favored in today's competitive job environment.

Organizational Skills

You not only have to be able to walk and chew gum at the same time, you need to be able to juggle cell phones and text while you do these things. It's complicated out there, and you have to be able to master the complexity.

To do so, strong organizational skills are a must. To effectively participate in a wide variety of tasks will require that you can keep track of yourself, your schedule, your electronic and paper files, and any number of other things you may need in a given field. You need to be able to prioritize — focusing on important projects, managing details, and developing step-by-step plans to accomplish your goals.

When you hit the big time, you'll have your laptop, netbook or iPad, and the latest handheld technology to help you manage day-to-day activities, but an organized thought process and the ability to keep your head above water on multiple projects at one time are of keen interest to employers. Multitasking rules the day. The good news here is that today's students are the ultimate multitaskers — but remember, it's *effective* multitasking that employers will be looking for.

A basic starting point here is effectively using a daily planner — if you don't already. Many schools today offer official planners, with key school-related dates already built into them. You can also use a system like the Franklin Covey planner, or create your own with an off-the-shelf planner from an office supply store. If you don't already manage your life with a planner, make the leap and start *now*. You may have to use a bit of trial and error to see what works for you, but you'll be far ahead in the long run if you manage your life with some type of organizational tool — the old-fashioned kind or an electronic version.

Most jobs also involve some type of project management. Inherent in "projects" is that there are numerous steps with some dependent on others. These usually involve diverse team members — all of whom must work in a synchronized manner to achieve a goal. There is a *lot* of complexity that you'll need to be able to manage.

Being organized will improve not only *your* productivity, but that of your staff and fellow team members.

Leadership

Employers want people who will be able to come in and make a difference. They want employees who can rally a team behind them and make things happen, people who can and will take their organization in fantastic new directions.

Now, don't let this one intimidate you. Nobody is expecting you to come in and run or restructure the company overnight. They just want people who, once they're settled in and understand the organization, will actively work to improve it and have the ability to come up with new ideas and turn them into reality. In simplified terms, they want people who will make things they are involved in "different" and "better" because they are a part of them.

True leadership is *not* about titles. There are many students who have fancy titles from college organizations that never truly *lead* those groups. They may run meetings but never do anything to improve the organization. If the group is not *different* or *better* because they have been a part of it, they haven't really led.

Related to this, a central principle of management today is empowering employees, giving them the freedom and flexibility to make a personal difference rather than micromanaging them. As a part of this, an effective manager needs to be able to be a very good "coach" — offering both positive and negative feedback (and developing future managers in that process).

Obviously, within the empowerment concept, employees who are leaders rather than simply followers are in high demand.

Inherent in strong leadership is being able to get others focused with you on a goal and working together to make that goal a reality. Directing, motivating, and training team members *and* actually producing meaningful positive results are core elements of successful leadership.

Logic

This characteristic is not as simple as it sounds. Some jobs require strong *analytical* ability. Others require *creative* thinking skills. Still others require long-term *strategic* planning or complex *problem-solving* ability. Regardless, raw smarts and the ability to think your way to a solution play a key role in the hiring decision. By the way, these are not always the easiest qualities to be able to identify in an interview.

Like it or not, your GPA will play a role in a recruiter's evaluation of your ability here, as will the perceived quality of your school. If the company is interviewing at your school, it obviously has some faith in the institution itself. If the company doesn't regularly interview there, they either don't view your school as a primary resource *or* they don't hire many students right out of college.

Most jobs also have some quantitative component to them, which often includes managing some kind of budget or performance metrics. You may not think you're a "numbers person" but you should *NOT* avoid any and all things numerical in college as most employers will want to know you're at least comfortable with the basics in this area.

Your logic will also be judged based on the quality of your answers to questions in the interview. Another interview style, a "case-based" approach, is designed to get at your skills here. You may be asked, for instance, how many street lights there are in Chicago. *Really!* If you are asked, will you be well-organized in your follow-up questions to get more information to allow you to make an intelligent estimate? Are your thoughts cohesive and concise? Are you logical and complete in your answer and rationale for it, or do you ramble on or never completely respond to the question? It does make a difference.

One final thought here. As much as you learn in college, you'll graduate knowing only a fraction of what you'll need to know to be successful in your career. Are you a "learner" by nature? Do you enjoy sharing what you learn? Smart people are even more valuable if they *want* to get smarter and will share information openly within the organization.

Effort

When the going gets tough, employers want someone who will rise to a challenge, not run from it. They want someone who will be willing to go the extra mile and make the personal sacrifice necessary to get the job done correctly and on time. And, they know a career is a marathon, not a

sprint. They want individuals who can get focused and then *stay* focused, going the distance and performing consistently for the organization over an extended period of time. Lots of people *talk* a big game. They want people who *play* one.

It is *VERY* easy to sit in an interview and say that you are hard working and will put forth any level of effort necessary to get the job done. It is equally easy for the recruiter not to believe you. A behavioral-based interview question like "What is the most difficult situation you have ever been in, and how did you work through it?" will help the recruiter get at this one. You can't fake an answer to a question like that. You either stepped up and got the job done… or you didn't.

What you have done — both in and out of the classroom — *should* prove that you have the motivation and drive that is so important to recruiters (and grad schools). Your overall record of achievement and the specific accomplishments you've had in the classroom, in your activities, and as a part of your work efforts will usually tell a recruiter all she needs to know on this one.

Group Skills

The "team" approach to running a business is fairly universal. Today, it's all about "collaborating" and "consensus-building." The smart but abrasive employee with a dominating style just doesn't do as well as he did even 10 years ago. Other team members won't give that type of individual consistent cooperation or 100% effort. Some people will actually work to undermine him. Therefore, more than ever, the ability to work effectively with others is critical to success.

And, this doesn't necessarily mean *leading* a team. It also means, when the situation calls for it, being an effective, contributing, *non-leading* team member. Yes, you not only need to know how to *lead*, you need to be able to *follow*. You need to be able to meaningfully contribute to team success without being the person in charge.

Once again, in an interview setting, *real* personal examples of how you have been an effective team member in the past will speak louder than general statements about how amazing you are in a team setting. It won't matter if you *tell* the recruiter you are effective. It is how you can *prove* that you have been a contributing team member that will make the difference.

By the way, building quality relationships is a key piece of this equation. Once people trust and believe in you (and you in them), things happen much more smoothly and efficiently. If you have negative relationships with team members based on bad history with them, getting things done will become a *LOT* more difficult. Firms — even very large ones — are smaller than you think, so building and sustaining relationships really matters. Building strong relationships is the only strategy that allows you to work effectively on teams and help your organization become successful.

Between the quality of your resume and your responses during the interview, the recruiter will walk away with a pretty good grasp of your skills in this area.

Entrepreneurship

The rate of change in the world is accelerating dramatically. In today's workplace, doing things "like we've always done them" is no longer something to celebrate. Unless you're selling something as antique, old, classic, or nostalgic, doing something "like we've always done it" means someone else is probably doing it faster, better, or more profitably.

The ability to adapt to change *quickly*, and the ability to *create* it are valued commodities in today's workplace. Too many employees today resist change because they are comfortable with the old way. The new way involves risk — risk of failure and extra work. That extra work may or may not pay off depending on whether or not the new way is truly a step forward. Are you willing to take that risk? Actually *embracing* change and being able to adapt quickly when a new approach is adopted makes you a strong potential contributor to an organization for decades to come.

Prospective employers are looking for concrete examples of your **Entrepreneurship**. They can be things you did related to your summer job at the ice cream shop or your sorority's intramural soccer team. In any scenario, they want to know you've changed something other than the channel on your TV or the order of songs in your favorite playlist on your iPod.

In a nutshell, that's what recruiters are looking for — the **Winning Characteristics**. The trick is to *prove,* in concrete ways, that you have developed these **Winning Characteristics** during your college career. And, I'm not talking about just a single example of how you have exhibited each characteristic. You'll want a variety of examples from different activities in different aspects of your life to prove that you have each of the seven.

Remember the acronym COLLEGE.

Addendum to the Winning Characteristics
Since the first printing of "Making College Count," there have been significant ethics scandals with devastating impact in

CAREER

COMMUNICATION | ORGANIZATION | LEADERSHIP | LOGIC | EFFORT | GROUP SKILLS | ENTREPRENEUR

American business. Ten years ago, it was generally *assumed* in the interview process that an individual was a person of character. Not any more. There is now a much stronger focus on ethics in the hiring process. The perception that you have strong ethics — and are an honest person who will try to do the right thing whenever possible — will not alone land you a dream job. *However*, the perception that you are, in any way, of shaky character or have a history of exhibiting bad judgment will immediately disqualify you for most jobs.

In American business, firms in a range of industries have basically evaporated based on illegal acts by key executives. Firms like Arthur Anderson and Enron used to be household names. Today, they no longer exist. So employers will look to better understand your moral compass — or lack thereof — in the interview process and when doing reference checks on you.

Also plan on a company doing a background check on you, googling you, looking at every online page you have posted on every social network site, even finding ways to see things that you had previously posted online. You *will* miss out on a great job if a potential employer thinks your Facebook page is inappropriate. Really. *Think* before you post *anything anywhere* online… you're creating a permanent record when you do.

Building These Characteristics

Now, before you get overwhelmed, get a headache, or give up before you even start, let me assure you of one thing. You *can* build all of these skills, put yourself in a position to *prove* you own them, *and* have a truly great time while you're in college. It's not as difficult and complex as you may think. Your academic experience, extracurricular activities, and employment environments are all loaded with opportunities. It's all about having a good plan — and executing that plan effectively.

You'll accumulate some examples of how you've exhibited the **Winning Characteristics** without even trying. You can create *many* more if you focus on building them.

> **Building the Winning Characteristics is key to building a successful future.**

What Your Grad School
is Looking For

Medical school?
Law school?
Business school?

You may have absolutely no idea what you plan to do after graduating from college. No problem. You may not have the slightest clue as to whether or not you'll continue your formal education. Not an issue. Or, you may know that you'll be continuing your education after receiving an undergraduate degree and that you won't be interviewing for your first job for at least six years. Given these possible scenarios, you may wonder if this book will apply to your life.

Regardless of your ultimate path, you still have a high hurdle to jump after undergraduate graduation. It may not be an employer, but you're going to have to impress *somebody*. You need a little more going for you than a heartbeat, a decent standardized test score, and a thick wallet to get accepted into a top graduate school program. And, while it may surprise you, the "judges" at those schools — admissions officers — do think a *LOT* like the employers discussed in the last chapter.

Are the Stanford University School of Medicine and a New York ad agency looking for all the same things in a candidate? Of course not, but the **Winning Characteristics** *are* important to both of these two dramatically different organizations.

Your demonstrated mastery of the **Winning Characteristics** will be of interest to any type of selection committee or interview team you'll face. They'll be the criteria used by the folks deciding if you will have the opportunity to be a part of their group, team, firm, practice, school, or company.

The days of a strong grade point average and a stellar test score being enough to get you into a top grad school are behind us. Even if it worked for a parent, relative or neighbor in the past, I promise, it will not work today.

> The world has changed, and so have the criteria for excelling in it.

CHAPTER 4
Some Basics

Time for some clichés.

"You have to crawl before you can walk."

"You have to walk before you can run."

The morsel of truth in these is that you do have to master basic skills before you can move on to advanced ones. And, because mastering the **Winning Characteristics** is a bit more challenging than learning to walk or run, the principles apply here as well.

Just a few more clichés.

"All work and no play makes Jack a dull boy."
(All play and no work makes Jack a dropout, by the way.)

"Everybody pays their dues."

"There's no free lunch."

Simply put, your willingness to manage work versus play and your commitment to "paying your dues" are *essential* to having a shot at success in college and in your future career(s). And, your ability to master the basics of goal setting and time management will be critical. A lot of your ability to prove that you possess the **Winning Characteristics** will

> You have to **master some basic skills** before moving to more advanced ones.

come from time you commit to building a successful future *in addition to* the hours it will take to get adequate grades.

The most fundamental goal for college is *survival*. Freshman year is dramatically different from anything you've ever experienced, particularly if you'll be living on your own for the first time. Realistic goal setting, exceptional time management, and the right mind-set will go a long way in ensuring you'll accomplish the survival fundamental.

> If you don't get past your first year, there's not much else to concern yourself with in this book.

Work Versus Play

College is a great time. Some would argue that your college years are the best years of your life. College *should* be a lot of fun. There's no doubt about it. *I had a great time in college*. But in spite of popular belief, there's life *after* college too. It can be pretty amazing if you've set yourself up for success during your college years.

The bad news is that you have to work for a living after you graduate. The good news is that the job can be a whole lot more enjoyable to you than your jobs in college. In fact, if you do what it takes to land your dream job coming out of college, you *should* actually enjoy work.

And, while you'll definitely have less free time after you graduate, you'll actually have some *money* in your pocket to pursue your hobbies and interests, be able to afford to go to professional sports and entertainment events, to support causes of interest to you, and travel to some fascinating places. In fact, even if you were fortunate enough to have some money in your pocket during college, it's nice to be able to spend your own money after graduation and be responsible to no one but yourself.

My point is that you don't have to try to have every bit of fun you will have in your entire life in college. Take advantage of the opportunities to enjoy your time in school. Make the most of it. Have fun! Just don't go so crazy doing it that you severely damage your ability to have fun after you graduate.

Remember the "Cold Hard Facts" section?

If you don't do what you need to in college to get the job done, you could easily (and will probably) join the ranks of the approximately one in two students who don't graduate (ACT,

2009). Or, you could be one of the two in five students who graduates and will take a job that doesn't require a college degree. Neither would be an optimal situation. Not for your career, not for your ego, and not for your bank account.

Said another way, by most standards, having to work two part-time jobs as a waiter after college to pay off your student loans would not classify as a "big win." It would, on the other hand, be a potential indicator that you may have been a bit too focused on fun during your days on campus. *Balance* is the key.

Let me share with you one other thought, one that is not particularly popular in some circles today. Nobody owes you anything. Not one thing. You get what you earn.

It is popular today to believe that there's a good living to be made by everyone and that the government and/or big corporations will take care of you. You *deserve* that, right? While it may feel at times like there will always be someone there to provide for you, it is simply not true. I'm sorry to be the bearer of bad news, but the sooner you have this revelation, the better off you'll be.

The reality is that you'll be graduating into a job market that is tougher and more competitive than ever before. Big companies are downsizing and tens of millions of baby boomers are currently camping out in the jobs you will want.

The good news is that it's still America, the "Land of Opportunity." It sounds a little cheesy to say that, but there *are* still amazing opportunities out there. Really. They may not be as obvious or as plentiful as you would like, but they do exist. You've just got to work hard and go after them.

The choice of how hard you'll work
to achieve success is yours and yours alone.

Paying Your Dues

It's an old expression, "Everybody pays their dues." It's how you get ahead. And you know what? It's true. And the sooner in life you start paying, the lower the amount of dues you'll ultimately pay to reach a given level of achievement. Underline it, highlight it, memorize it, or write it on your wall. To get ahead, you must pay your dues. And the sooner you do, the lower the toll. Remember, there is no free ride.

Think of "dues-paying" as an opportunity, not a task. It is a chance, through hard work, to propel yourself to a different level. If you choose to do it, the results can be amazing.

As I mentioned, I was informed quite clearly at my high school senior awards assembly that I had *not* paid my dues. I was not the recipient of one of the many scholarships awarded.

Having an unspectacular grade point average and almost no extracurricular activities, I just wasn't one of those "ideal students" that every college was looking to throw money at to get them to attend.

The decision I made that day — to pay my dues in college and do whatever it took to stand out — was the smartest decision I've made in my life. I didn't realize it at the time, but college is the best time in life to pay your dues. The environment is ideal for it and you have so much time on your hands that you can pay your dues *and* still have the time of your life. The same opportunity is much less likely after college.

It is important to mention, though, that if you do *not* make the personal decision to pay your dues in college, your life will not end. You *will*, however, have a *STEEP* hill to climb after graduation to catch up to the people who did. Unfortunately, it will almost certainly include taking a job or two for which a degree is not required.

Looking at things from another perspective, you might also simply aspire to be "average." I've had students

honest
enough to
tell me that and I
really respected their
candor. They want to
get a job, work enough to
be "effective" — and not a
minute more. They want a
relaxed, stress-free lifestyle. There's nothing wrong with that — if
that's truly what you want. My hunch is that your perspective on
this will change as you get older, get married, and have kids to
financially support. You may also rethink it when less qualified
people are getting promoted to be your boss because they
outworked you. That said, *every* person is different and choosing
your goals is up to *you*.

The bottom line here? If you choose to pay your dues, you will
dramatically increase the quality and quantity of opportunities
available to you. It's that simple.

On a personal level, I've watched friends work 24/7 to try to play catch-up after college. It did not happen easily. It did not happen quickly. It did not happen without great personal sacrifice. And for some, it did not happen at all. They simply never caught up.

Also worth mentioning is that this dues-paying job after college will not necessarily be a great deal of fun and will most likely require night and weekend work. You'll need to truly *excel* in that position to prove to your next recruiter that you've grown up and become a more mature, responsible person since your "blow off" days in college.

One more point. Don't count on your manager at this job to be supportive or particularly helpful in your endeavors. He may or may not be a decent manager, may or may not have a college degree, may or may not like people with college degrees, and may be intimidated and feel that you're a threat to him. You just don't know.

I know this is a worst case, nightmare scenario. It's also not completely unrealistic either. Hopefully, you get the idea.

> It is much, much, much easier to pay your dues in college than afterwards!

Setting Some Goals

"It's a dream until you write it down.
Then it's a goal."

There is very little
that is as simple or
powerful as sitting down
and writing out your goals.
It sounds so easy that it

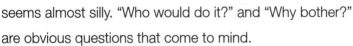

seems almost silly. "Who would do it?" and "Why bother?"
are obvious questions that come to mind.

Well, you're going to have to trust me (at least a little bit) on this
one. Committing your goals to paper can be incredibly powerful
if you do it with some degree of thoughtfulness and then post
the goals in a place where you'll see them on a regular basis.

There are three parts to the process. I've just touched on steps two and three. They are the easy parts.

2. Write them down
3. Keep them in a place where you can't help but see them regularly

Step one is the hard part. It goes as follows:

1. Set the goals

To accomplish this, you need to have some feel for what you want in the short and long term.

It's better to *start* by looking out into the distant future. Where do you want to be in 10 years? More specifically, where do you want to be personally and professionally at that point? Even if you don't yet have a feel for what career direction you'd like to pursue, you certainly should be able to put together a mental picture of what type of lifestyle you'd like to have at that point in your life.

A 10-year Look

Answering the following questions may help:

- Where will you live?
- What type of home/condo/apartment will you have?
- What will you do for fun?
- Will you be single or married?
  (Obviously someone else gets to vote on this one, too.)

- Where will you be traveling?
- What kind of physical condition will you be in?
  How will you accomplish this?
- What kind of community service work
  might you be doing, if any?
- What type of work will you be doing?
- How much money will you have saved, if any?
- Are you really willing to pay your dues
  to achieve success?

Two hints here.

First, the lifestyle you want is probably significantly more expensive than you would imagine. When you start paying for glamorous things like groceries, cell phone bills, car loans, car insurance, utilities, gas to get to/from work, etc., the costs add up very quickly.

Second, life is a building process (see the "Paying Your Dues" section). You probably won't go from a minimum wage job to a highly lucrative career overnight. You'll need to understand the steps in the process that will allow you to get to that dream job.

Spend some time creating a clearer vision of where you'd like to be long-term. Candidly, it's hard. The most difficult part might be deciding how you personally define "success" and how *BIG* you want to think. I think defining success is a very personal thing. There are no right or wrong answers — just right and wrong answers for you. And, do you want to set lofty goals and do the work to get there — or is *average* good enough for you? Good question, isn't it?

If you were a student in my class at Miami University, I would require that you write out a 10-page, 10-year life plan. It's not a simple task as it involves a lot of thinking about not just where you want to be but the specific steps in the process you'll need to complete to actually get there. As a part of that process, you'll set some shorter-term goals. I'll spend a bit more time on that later in the book.

I would also suggest that you think *BIG* in setting your goals — really *BIG*. Someone has to be wildly successful, why not you? Generally speaking, if you don't think *BIG*, you'll set goals too conservatively and won't push yourself as hard as you are capable of pushing to achieve your *true* potential. When you read the stories of truly successful people, they weren't all child prodigies or straight A students in grades K-12. Many hit their stride in college. Again, *someone* has to be amazingly successful. Why not *YOU*?

> How great will you choose to be?

Managing Your Time

Time management. It sounds kind of boring, but it's critical to making the most of your college experience. Hopefully, you're moving in the direction of setting some challenging goals for yourself. Time management will help you achieve them.

As a starting point, you need to realize that you have a *LOT* of time on your hands in college. *A LOT* probably doesn't even do it justice. An *unbelievable* amount or a *ridiculous* amount may be more accurate. If you get eight hours of sleep per night (unlikely), that will give you 16 hours a day to work with! If you get a more typical six hours, you'll have 18 hours a day to work with. That's a tremendous amount of time.

Not to get overly technical, but 18 hours a day is 126 hours a week. If you're taking a typical 16 hours a week of classes,

that leaves 110 hours to study, work, volunteer, pursue extracurricular activities, have ridiculous amounts of fun, and take care of life's necessities (like eating, laundry, etc.). Even if you decide that every Thursday, Friday, and Saturday from 6 p.m. on will be fully dedicated to fun, you still have over 80 hours left.

Just in case you're not convinced, let's look at it another way. In high school, you probably left the house at 7 a.m. and did not get home until 4 p.m. or later. If you did that five days a week, you put in 45 hours a week. If you're taking a full course load in college, you're taking 16 hours of classes. Even if you add travel time to/from classes, extracurricular or volunteer activities, and/ or a part-time job to the mix, most people have a LOT more time on their hands in college than they did in high school.

So, while it might not always feel this way, for most of you, *you'll have more time on your hands than you ever have before or ever will again.*

Some thoughts on how to manage that time.

First, schedule early classes. Take 8 a.m. classes if you can get up easily, 9 a.m. if you can't. Early classes will force you to get out of bed at a reasonable time, not unlike you did in high school (or what your future employer will expect from you). You'd be amazed at how easy it is to sleep until 10:30 a.m. if your first class starts at 11 a.m. If you don't think you can consistently make 8 a.m. classes (although you really ought to be able to), go for classes at 9 a.m. Even I could make it to a 9 a.m. class. You can too.

And, of course, when you schedule these early classes, go to them — every day!

Second, study between classes. Often you'll have an hour or two to kill between classes. Get into the routine of making valuable use of these time slots. It's not that tough. Go to the library and put those hours to work for you. It's amazing the number of ways that people waste time between classes. With all of the portable electronics at your disposal, you can waste time from virtually anywhere! And realistically, there aren't that many *amazing* things you can be doing from 10 a.m. to noon on a Tuesday morning so you won't be missing much by studying.

Third, study after class before dinner. This seems rather obvious, but you'd be blown away at how many college students spend their afternoons watching ESPN, soap operas, and reruns of bad TV shows. It's incredible. They'll sit there for most of the day for weeks at a time. Spending hours a day on social networking sites or texting would also *not* classify as brilliant time management. If you tracked how many hours you spend per week in front of a computer screen doing non-essential things (things other than homework, research, etc), my bet is that it would be at least 15 hours per week — and for many of you more than 20.

By the way, studying in front of the TV — trying to have fun and study all at once — does *not* make you a time management wizard. You'll get little or nothing from the studying and miss about half of the show. It's the epitome of bad time management.

Big time waster, bad idea

Fourth, when you study, FOCUS. Make it quality study time, not social time. Study in a quiet environment and at a high level of intensity. Personally, I wouldn't even listen to music unless it's purely instrumental (i.e. no lyrics), and you're doing it to drown out some background noise. If you maximize the *quality* of the study time, you can minimize the *quantity* of time needed to get the job done.

In general, make the most of extra hours available to you *during* the day. During the day, the temptations not to study are fewer and much less exciting and this approach will free up your evenings for extracurriculars and more legitimate fun.

Here's one more simple calculation. If you take 16 hours a week of classes starting at 9 a.m. each day, take an hour lunch, go to the library between and after classes, finish at 5 p.m., and spend an hour getting from place to place during the day, you'll have put in 19 hours at the library in a week. That is a tremendous amount of study time on a week-in, week-out basis. If you start at 8 a.m. and spend only a half an hour on lunch, you'll have put in more than 25 hours of study time. *Welcome to the Dean's List!*

With this approach, your nights and weekends will be study-free (other than before midterms or finals), and you'll have a serious head start towards a strong grade point average. Sounds pretty good, doesn't it?

Looking at the bigger picture, you should manage your time from a total semester standpoint. Get or create some type of good daily semester schedule planner. Each professor will provide a syllabus (schedule) outlining what material will be covered each week, when major papers are due, and when tests will occur. Knowing in advance will allow you to get a head start on some of the work to avoid a "train wreck" during those time frames.

Before I end this section, let me throw out a thought about holding down a job while in college. If you need to work while school is in session, take everything I've said about the importance of time management and multiply it by three. Your task is significantly more difficult. However, it *is* still manageable if you understand that time is your single most precious commodity and act accordingly. You just can't waste it.

You'll find an entire chapter on working during college later in the book. Holding down a job will require you to have a sharper focus on time management, but it doesn't have to destroy your opportunity for success.

> College is great. Make the most of it while you're there and life after college will be great too.

Surviving Year One

If *surviving* is not on your list of freshman goals, perhaps you should reconsider. In 2009, more than three out of 10 freshmen did not achieve this goal and did not return to school as sophomores. That's a big number and a huge waste of time and money.

In my freshman residence hall, our resident advisor (an upperclassmen who is paid to live in a dorm to keep order and provide student-to-student guidance and perspective) called us together during our first week. He told the 40 of us to look around. He said that five of us would probably not make it to second semester and that 10 of us would not make it to sophomore year. I thought he was just trying to scare us. He wasn't.

Six guys weren't back for second semester. A dozen never saw their sophomore year. These guys were not stupid. In fact, most of them were pretty bright. They just lacked balance. I'll share with you the story of two of them to make the point.

The guys were Spaceman and Worm (18-year-old guys can come up with some odd nicknames). Both went to more than their share of parties and had several *years* worth of fun during their first semester. Worm stayed out late, slept in late, and played a whole lot of hoops. Spaceman stayed out late, got up early, left the dorm and disappeared all day — every day. Worm flunked out. Spaceman made the Dean's list.

What was the difference? Spaceman went to class. We also found out later that he spent his time between classes and in the afternoon at the library. There was no shortage of college fun in his life. He just had a little bit of balance. He was a master of time management.

There was one other common feature of all the "one semester

wonders" I knew. They dug themselves an incredible hole in the first six weeks. They didn't go to class regularly. They didn't do their assignments. They didn't do the necessary reading. They thought they could catch up later "like they did in high school." The hole they dug was so deep that it was close to impossible to get out. And they didn't.

Make a commitment to survive the first year. Start by not getting buried your first six weeks. Be a "geek." Read your assignments. Do your homework problems twice. Go to *every* class. You or your parents paid a *LOT* for you to be able to go to a class — so don't throw that money down a hole. Overstudy for quizzes and tests. Is overstudy even a word? Regardless of whether it is or not, you know what I mean so *DO IT*.

Survive the first six weeks. Then try to survive for the whole semester. Then go for the whole year. You *will* have to do some serious work to handle a college course load, but you'll learn how to manage it effectively if you take this approach.

Also worth mentioning is that a reasonable course load will help. Don't try to complete a four-year program in three years or get a jump start on a triple major unless you have a track record that would indicate that doing so is a reasonable proposition. And, don't be afraid to put an easy course on the list. It can help you keep your head above water while you're battling a killer calculus or chemistry class.

If you've loaded up on AP or IB credit in high school, it's okay to take a *slightly* lighter load for your first semester to allow yourself to settle in and establish a routine that works for you. Lighter loads *every* semester mean a longer time to graduate so please don't follow this one out the window. It will be expensive and reflect poorly on you in the long term.

Let's, for a minute, get a little loftier with your goals. Let's talk about not just surviving your freshman year. Let's talk about actually doing well. Somebody has to get the A's and B's in a given class. The professor can't flunk everyone. So, it might as well be you who gets the A, right? Why not? Beyond simply being allowed to come back for a second year, there are a number of other *major* advantages to getting off to a fast start.

First, once you get some decent grades, you'll know you're capable of more. You'll get a bit more comfortable with the idea of success in college and settle in quickly toward making that success a reality. A strong start out of the gate is a huge confidence builder.

Second, a strong academic performance will open doors to some significant opportunities. From student government to the campus newspaper, from volunteer activities to ROTC, the groups you want to join will *want* you to join them. If they think you can barely handle your current course load, they will not think you'll be able to make a meaningful contribution to their group.

Organizations may tell you that grades do not play a big role in their decision-making process. They'll do that right up to the moment when they decide to deny your application and instead opt for candidates who are effectively managing their academic requirements. That's a fancy way of saying that people with good grades are going to get the spots in selective organizations that *you* want to join. As we'll discuss later, these clubs and organizations will be critical to your interviewing success.

Let's also look at how you'll help your cause in terms of future employment with good first-year grades. When you start interviewing for internships your junior year, you'll have only *two* years of grades in your cumulative average. When you create your resume as a senior, you'll only have *three* years behind you. Your freshman grades will have a tremendous impact on your GPA. If you pursue an internship between your sophomore and junior years, you'll interview with only your freshman grades. Your freshman grades are *incredibly* important.

If your freshman grades are strong, they will pull your cumulative average up throughout college. On the other hand, if you get a 2.0 as a freshman, even a strong 3.5 your sophomore year will leave you with a 2.75 going into internship interviews. If you follow with a respectable 3.2 your junior year, you'll still only have a 2.9. Had you rallied to a 3.0 your freshman year, you'd be in decent shape with a cumulative 3.2 with the 3.5 sophomore and 3.2 junior performance mentioned above. If you had a 3.8 your freshman year, you'd be looking at a 3.65 after sophomore year and a 3.5 cumulative average after junior year. A strong freshman performance can be a *BIG* help.

By the way, these strategies apply equally as well if you are in a two-year degree/certificate program at a community college or technical school, in a 2+2 program—meaning you are attending a community college and plan to transfer and get a four-year degree, are in an online program, or any four-year college or university. Freshman year is crucial—no matter what school environment you find yourself in.

Let me repeat this message: A strong academic performance in your freshman year can pay unbelievable positive dividends for you. So make a commitment to success in the first six weeks, then in the first semester, and do your best from there.

> Remember, playing catch up is not a winning option at the college level.

CHAPTER 5
Getting the Grades

To ensure you will have great career opportunities coming out of college, your GPA is where it all begins.

Getting good grades alone will not convince potential employers

Grades will help get you an interview so you can showcase the many strengths you possess.

that you have all of the **Winning Characteristics** they are looking for. It will, however, let them know that you have some mix of **Logic** and **Organizational Skills**. It will let them know you're willing to put forth **Effort** to achieve your goals. Good grades will earn you the interviews for the jobs you desire. If you don't have the grades to get the interview you can't showcase those many other strengths you possess!

If you don't get decent grades, you're dead before you get
out of the starting blocks. It will be extremely tough to get
an interview for an outstanding job. And, even if you do, put
yourself in the recruiter's shoes. Why should he believe that you
are intelligent and mature enough to do the job for his company
if you haven't done your job particularly well for the past four
years? Go back to the behavioral-based interview concept. The
answer, therefore, is that he *won't* believe you.

And, if you were the recruiter, would you want to go back to
your boss and tell him or her that your best candidate has a 2.4
average? I don't think so.

No individual thing you'll learn in this section is the one magic
bullet that will make college easy. Taken as a whole, though, this

information can and should *significantly* improve your academic performance. Hopefully, you will have also mastered some effective study techniques in high school. If you have, use them in college. It's really all about what works for *you*.

Along with helping you get good grades, good study techniques can also make you more efficient so you don't have to spend your *entire* college experience in the library.

After all, there is more
to college than studying.

How Good Do Your Grades Have to Be?

I cannot be too emphatic here. *YOU DO NOT NEED A 4.0, STRAIGHT A AVERAGE TO SUCCEED AFTER COLLEGE.* It's just not necessary to be academically *perfect*. On the other hand, if you're not willing to work any harder than it will take to get a 2.2, don't even bother to go to college. With this type of performance, you will most likely not improve your career opportunities relative to a high school graduate.

With a weak academic performance, you'll be almost certain to take a job that's a nightmare for you after graduation. So either plan to do better than a 2.2 — actually better than a 2.5 — or save yourself the trouble involved in going to college and find a way to learn a skill that will get you some kind of job immediately after high school. Or, consider the military as the way to build skills to prepare you for your career. It's not right for everyone —

but it can be a very good choice if it's a fit for you.

While these GPA targets are rough guidelines (and there certainly are exceptions), you can typically get a good job out of college in a decent economy with a 3.0 cumulative average and a 3.3 average in your major. You put yourself into contention for a GREAT job with a 3.5 overall and a 3.5 in your major. In a weak economy, it might take numbers a bit better than these to get the job you want. Employers will be hiring fewer people so they can afford to be a bit more selective. In a strong economy, you may be able to get away with a slightly weaker performance. But, regardless of the economy, do you really want to settle for a weak GPA and put yourself at risk?

The key point here is that good numbers will *get you an interview* and will put the recruiter in a positive frame of mind when she meets you. *They simply get you in the game. Grades alone will not get you the job.* There are too many people with solid grades out there, just too much competition. As I mentioned, good grades will effectively sell your ability to think (**Logic**). They will probably also reinforce the fact that you are **Organized** and motivated to succeed (**Effort**), but that's about as far as it goes. You will need to show that you have *all* of the **Winning Characteristics**. Three of seven will not get it done.

On the flip side, if you lack respectable grades, you probably won't even get an interview. And even if you do get an interview,

You don't need to LIVE at the library.

you'll have a steep uphill battle to really get a recruiter's attention. A recruiter will talk to approximately 16 students in a given day. If you don't have the grades, you're certainly not her lead candidate going into interview day.

If you're planning to go into a sales or marketing related position, you may think you don't *really* need the grades. You'll just need to be able to "sell yourself" well in an interview. Right? *Wrong!* These fields are now much more complex than they have been historically, and the ability to think strategically and do complex numerical analysis is more critical than ever. Again, if you can't get the grades in college, why should an employer believe you could perform in his organization? It's a competitive job market. The employer just doesn't need to take the risk.

Even if you plan to pursue a career in a technical or numbers-based field like information technology, finance, or engineering, there's still a lot more to getting hired these days than just good grades. Grades are still *VERY* important. They're just not the complete picture. Firms want well-rounded individuals, not just someone who can get a 3.96 by living in the library.

One final point. If you are a gifted individual capable of that elusive 3.96, I would suggest that you get even *more* focused on extracurricular activities. Spend the extra time rounding yourself out. Even if your grades slip to a 3.6 or 3.7, there will still be no concern about your intellectual firepower. You're smart! But remember, lots of people are smart. *What makes you more than smart?* What you do with that extra time could make the difference on interview day.

Companies and grad schools *do* want smart applicants, but they want more than mere *brainiacs*. If you have a 3.96 but have done nothing but study for four years, what exactly do you plan to talk about in the interview? Besides, your participation in extracurricular activities will *prove* that you didn't spend 12 hours a day, seven days a week, with your face in a book to get your grades.

Resumes, by the way, won't get nearly the attention you think they will. Generally, your carefully crafted resume will get about 10 seconds of attention — *just 10 seconds* — before the individual with your future in her hands decides to reject you or give you a shot at an interview. A GPA above her undisclosed "hurdle rate" will get you a look beyond the 10-second initial cut.

The following sections will assist you in getting the kind of grades I'm talking about. It will take some work, but it's definitely possible and worth the effort.

Understanding Professors

WAKE UP! This is one of the most critical chapters in the book.

Professors are people. They have personalities. They have egos. They develop relationships, and sometimes, yes, they even show compassion. They are all different and understanding them is critical.

It can be extremely beneficial to you. Don't underestimate this.

Most children start figuring out how to get what they want from adults by age two. They are very good at it by age six and have honed the skill to perfection by third grade. While they don't *always* get what they want, kids certainly know which buttons to push to have the best possible chance of getting what they want. A part of the reason that children are so effective at this is that they understand their audience. Children understand what their parents want, and they know how to give mom and dad what *they* want so that the children can get what *they* want.

Perhaps it makes sense to also understand your professors.

Think for a minute about what would make someone choose to become a professor. It will help you think about them in the proper light as you consider how to interact with them.

You would choose to become a professor, I think, because you had a passion for a subject area. You may also enjoy sharing that passion with other people and might even enjoy being in a relaxed/flexible campus setting and interacting with young, bright minds. And you would, I hope, be reasonably smart.

Professors think they are true experts in their subject areas. Fortunately, most are. Unfortunately, a few aren't. Regardless, the key insight here is that a professor, believing he is an expert in his field, is going to lecture on the subject matter he thinks is most important. And, if he lectures on specific topics, he'll test on them too. That seems obvious to me… but apparently is not to many students. Let me explain.

In most cases, your professor's name will not be on the spine

The key is probably NOT the books.

of the textbook for that class. She didn't write it, may not have personally chosen the book, and may or may not even like it. She probably feels like she has a better sense of what is important for you to learn in a class than the author of some book she has been told to use in the class by her department head. And, the more selective the school, the bigger the egos, and the more this phenomenon can sometimes exist.

Think about it. If the professor didn't write the book, studying it astutely to make up for missing five classes will be futile. It may not even cover the same material! *You'll surely crash and burn.*

YOU HAVE TO GO TO CLASS! And while you're in class, don't spare the ink. Take *lots* of notes to capture the key lecture points!

On the other hand, if your professor wrote the book, this obviously changes things quite a bit. The book becomes the focal point for that class. If your professor believed her thoughts were important enough to put in writing, you can bet she will lecture and test from her book.

Now that we've established the importance of your focus on the lecture material, it follows that you absolutely have to go to class and be attentive. I know I sound like somebody's mom or dad when I say this, but you do need to suck it up, go to class, and stay awake when you get there.

Blowing off class and borrowing someone's notes isn't the answer either. If you can actually read what they wrote, can you understand what the notes mean? What was the professor's area of emphasis? Which point  did she repeat three times? What question did she promise would be on the test? (This happens a lot more than you would think.) Borrowing notes to make up for sleeping late just doesn't work. Believe me, I've tried it. It's definitely better than nothing, but it's just not the same as being there.

And, of course, if a professor says something three or four times, she obviously thinks it's important. Write it down *TWICE*. Put a circle around it. Put a star next to it. *Somehow* highlight the fact that it was heavily emphasized. You *will* see it again on exam day.

Let me share another thought related to professors' mind-sets and students skipping or sleeping through class. It makes them mad — really mad. They are willing to share their wisdom with you by teaching. It is their life's work. You, by not showing up physically or mentally, are telling them that you really don't care what they have to say. Not a brilliant idea.

As a side note, many professors will drop your grade in a class (or flunk you) if you miss too many classes. Most will tell you what their policy is on this at the beginning of the semester — but don't count on that disclosure. For my class, I give students my cell phone number and e-mail address and tell them to contact me in advance of the class if they're going to miss a class — or they're going to have a *major* problem. My theory on this is that if I'm going to prepare the class, drive an hour to campus, and deliver a great session, I expect them to be there as well unless they have a good reason for missing. Seems reasonable to me. If they miss the class without giving me the courtesy of a call or an e-mail ahead of time, they fail my class. Really. When you get a job after college you can't just "no show" for work. Why should you be able to "no show" for my class? Did I mention that professors don't like it when you miss their classes?

If you're going to show up for class, *PARTICIPATE*. Many students, particularly freshmen and sophomores, think that professors are intimidating and unapproachable. They're afraid that the professor will find out how *little* they actually know if they speak up and ask a question. They also value their fellow students' class time (more than is necessary) and don't want to waste it with a "stupid" question.

If you're confused in class, stop the train! Ask the question. You've paid a lot of money to be there. Don't be embarrassed to get clarification on an issue. You've heard this before, but other people probably really do have the same questions as you do. And because in most subjects the next point builds on the last one, once you're lost, you're just going to become more and more confused as the class progresses. So go ahead, ask the question! Now, if you've asked several questions and just aren't getting it, let the professor proceed and go see her at "office hours," time formally set aside for helping students in need of additional assistance.

Going to class, asking questions, and going to office hours offer other advantages. They let professors know that you care, that you're a serious student who is giving his or her best effort. Professors can tell if you have a genuine interest in the subject area they have chosen as their life's work. It's the students who do this who often get a break if they're on the bubble between two grades. In many cases, grades aren't given just by the numbers. Effort does count.

Some additional thoughts on office hours. They are set up specifically for you to go ask questions. Take advantage of this opportunity throughout the semester. The professor sits at office hours with no visitors for weeks at a time. Then, the day before a test, half the class tries to get in to get a question answered. Obviously this doesn't always work out too well. You'll spend an hour in line, wasting precious study time. It still may be better than not going at all, but it is terribly inefficient. If you have questions, go regularly. Don't wait until the day before the test!

By the way, when you go, be organized. Have specific questions written out to guide the discussion. Be efficient with the professor's time. If you're just going to "chat" and earn some "brownie points," it will be obvious… and you won't earn any.

Grade trends can count, too. If your professor knows you've been giving it your all and you've had a C, a B and an A respectively on tests going into finals, you may want to try to negotiate with her before the final to give you an A for the class if you can pull an A on her cumulative final.

In some cases, she'll take you up on it.

Even if she doesn't, she'll remember you if you're "on the bubble" between two grades after the final.

If it's finals week and she has never seen you before (at office hours or actively participating in class), you can forget any type of negotiation. You're probably going to get what the numbers dictate.

There are other advantages to developing a positive relationship with your instructors. When it comes time to pursue your dream job, they can be great friends to have. They tend to be fairly well connected in their fields. In fact, corporate recruiters who are alumni of the school will often call their favorite professors to find out who their top students are prior to setting up their interview schedules. Professors can also be excellent sources of letters of recommendation for graduate schools or jobs. These letters can give you a leg up, particularly if you want to get an interview with a company that's not coming to your school.

A final point on relationships with professors — be sincere. If you think that buddying up with professors is a license to slack off in their classes and still get decent grades, you're going to learn a painful lesson. You're not going to do well. I am embarrassed to admit that a friend of mine from high school used to buy gifts for his college professors as a "bribe" for better grades. He was amazed when he found out it didn't work. I was amazed that he ever thought it might!

If you haven't been to class for months and/or haven't uttered a word to the professor the entire semester, you'll also strike out if you show up the week before finals to sell him on how hard you're trying. He wasn't born yesterday and will see you coming a mile away.

Before ending this chapter, I would be remiss if I didn't discuss professors with intimidating styles. They're out there and you'll probably end up sitting in a few of their classrooms in spite of your best efforts to avoid them. I'll break these fine folks into two categories, the "Stretchers" and the "Breakers."

The Stretchers are actually great — really. They want to prepare you for the "real world" by teaching you as much as they possibly can. They'll put you on the spot with tough questions in class. If you're zoning out in their class, the next query is guaranteed to come your way. They'll push on you, challenging your responses to see if you'll effectively stand up for your point of view or if you'll crumble at the first opportunity to do so. That said, they're generally good-natured people. They've just chosen

Good profs may stretch you a bit.

this teaching strategy to get the most they can from you.

The key for the Stretchers will be to see if you can support yourself confidently in class or in answering test questions with relevant facts from the course. In their minds, your future boss is going to do it so why not give you a little experience in this area while you're still in school. They may also make their exams extremely challenging, resulting in pitifully low class averages — often like 50% or 55%. They believe that if they make you reach for the stars, that while you may not get there, you'll get a lot closer than if you had shot for a lesser goal. Fortunately, these professors understand the concept of the curve and of a typical distribution of grades (i.e., 15% of the class gets an A, 30% get a B, etc). Stretchers aren't out to destroy you (or your grade point average). They're just out to make you the best you can be. Frankly, I think it's a valid philosophy.

The Breakers, on the other hand, are generally unhappy with the world and want to share that sentiment with all their *lucky* students. They are generally tenured professors (which means it's almost impossible to fire them) and are sometimes just biding their time until retirement — which may be five or 25 years away. You'll most likely experience their charming dispositions within the first couple weeks of their classes. They don't want to stretch you; they want to break you — *if* you're breakable.

My advice is not to be combative with these types. You'll lose. Just stay off their black lists, hold your tongue, and do the best that you can. Just be reassured that they can't flunk the entire class, in spite of the fact that they may threaten to do so. The other good news is that there are *very* few of these folks in the profession. I encountered only two of them in my four years of school. Considering that you'll have more than 40 professors during four years of college, you just need to know they're out there and manage them properly when you can't avoid them.

> Understand how your professors think.
> Spend the time to get to know them.
> It's worth the effort.

Class Selection Strategy

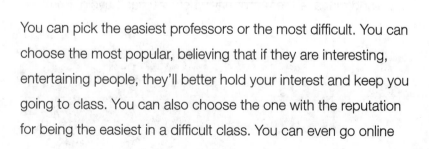

Class selection is something that should be done with careful consideration. There are several potential strategies to utilize. Your approach will have a major impact on your grades *and* the knowledge you take away from your college experience.

You can pick the easiest professors or the most difficult. You can choose the most popular, believing that if they are interesting, entertaining people, they'll better hold your interest and keep you going to class. You can also choose the one with the reputation for being the easiest in a difficult class. You can even go online today and get student ratings of professors rather than simply relying on the advice of a friend who's an upperclassman.

I suggest a combination of these strategies. I would recommend *challenging* professors within your major — not necessarily the ones with the reputation for flunking half the class, but the *stretchers*, the teachers with a reputation for being most knowledgeable and pushing their students. Your grade point average will survive. A professor who is trying to truly educate you and help you grow personally has no great incentive or desire to destroy your GPA.

Why should you subject yourself to challenging professors? Well, if you want to get a job related to your major after college *and* perform well in that job, you'll want to actually learn something in these classes. If you don't, you're asking for trouble. Your future employer will expect you to know at least "a little" about what they hired you to do because you have — to their knowledge — studied within that field for several years.

In fact, if you try to take the easy road early in your major, you'll probably have problems even before graduation.

Classes in a major tend to build on each other. So if you take the easy professor in Economics 201 and 202, you may have a serious problem when you get to Economics 301 if only a demanding professor is teaching the class. He won't try to reteach you what you're supposed to know. He'll pick up where he thinks you left off, and if you don't have a solid foundation after a year of entry level classes, you'll be in a real jam.

You'll obviously also want to take classes required by the school and within your major on the recommended timetable, filling out your schedule with elective options based on your interests. These elective classes (optional classes not specifically required to graduate in your major) will be taken for the most part during your junior and senior years. Which choices are right for you will be a little more obvious to you at that time.

Look at the possibility of a double major or picking up a minor when you make class selections. In some cases you can pick up a related minor with the addition of just a few classes. A second major that is similar to your current major may also be a lot less work than you would anticipate. You'll get to take fewer diverse elective classes, but it will improve your marketability in your future job hunt. I'm not saying you need a minor or a second major, but you should at least understand what your options are and know that a lot of students pursue this approach these days.

In required classes outside of your major, I would recommend a slightly less rigorous and somewhat more controversial approach. I'll call it *Easy Street*. If a history class is a requirement and two offered are of similar interest, take the easier one or the one you know has a professor who is not as demanding. In short, outside

your major, take classes that will help your GPA — not damage it. And remember, you *should* also have challenging classes in your major that semester and meaningful extracurricular activities. You're taking *Easy Street* for balance — not so you can play more video games.

Within the *Easy Street* approach, let common sense prevail. If a class you think you'll find really interesting appears to be a bit more challenging than a class that will bore you to tears, take the interesting class. It will be easier for you given your inherent interest.

Just don't take a physics class for engineering majors to meet a random science requirement. And remember, everyone has different interests. A good friend who loves European history may have thought a Russian art class was a breeze — a great way to knock off a humanities requirement. You, on the other hand, may be so bored that you fall asleep at your desk on a daily basis and struggle to get a C.

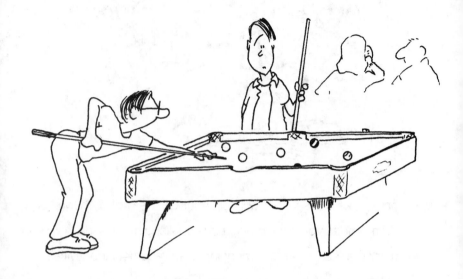

This is probably all the physics you will need.

One of the classes I took to fulfill my science requirements was Physics in Sports. It was very manageable, allowed me to spend more time on classes that were more meaningful to my career direction, and had no negative effect on my grade point average. I got an A and have never stumbled in my career due to a lack of strong physics knowledge! I did take a nutrition class for dietetics majors because I was genuinely interested in learning about the subject matter. It was a hard class and a gross violation of the *Easy Street* philosophy. I was interested in the subject matter, though, so I happily spent the time necessary to do well in the class. The decision to take a difficult class because of strong personal interest in the subject matter can be a great choice. Just plan to spend time on it, or plan to hurt your GPA.

Don't be afraid to utilize your pass/fail option. At some schools you can take a limited number of classes and receive credits for them but receive no grades as long as you get C's in the classes. Technically, a D grade is a passing grade, but at most schools, you'll need a C to be successful in a pass/fail class.

If there's a subject area outside of your major that you'd like to learn about without great risk to your GPA, the pass/fail option represents an outstanding opportunity. You don't want the C you might get in Wine Tasting 301 (which could actually be a challenging course if you're covering "The Geography of Wine") to hurt your grade point average. You'd be amazed at how many people get burned this way. The professors of those types of fun classes are working hard to legitimize them. If they don't, at some point the classes will be eliminated — and their jobs with them. They have no credibility if they give everyone A's.

Pass/fail is also a good strategy to pursue for a class or two outside your major during a quarter or semester when you are taking several extremely difficult and time consuming classes within your major. It helps even the load.

The best pass/fail strategy I have found is to ace the tests during the term and, *if you need to*, slide by on the final once you've locked up your C average or better so you get a "passing" grade. If you get off to a strong start and get a couple of A's or B's, you might be able to spend only an hour or two studying for the final — during a week when your time is of tremendous value to you. Your early success *should* provide some cushion on the final. So, you'll still receive a passing grade for the class regardless of your performance on the final.

Another important point. If you desperately want or need to get into a class and find it full or "closed," don't give up. As a fall back, sign up for an alternate class. Then go talk to the professor of the class you want and tell him you really want to take his class. Many professors have the ability to allow an extra student or two into their classes. If you are genuinely eager to take the class and it shows, talking with the professor about your interest might just give you the opportunity to do so.

If this does not work, go to the class. Other students may drop the class (which will open up a spot) or the professor may just make room for one more if he sees you at the first several classes and you remind him of your interest — without becoming a pest, of course. But, do register for and attend the other class until you are successful in working your way into your first-choice class. After you are, you can drop the alternate. Just don't get caught a class short!

A related part of good class selection strategy will be effective *professor* selection. How do you know which professors will best fit your strategy? Good question. You won't right away. But over time, by talking to fellow classmates and upperclassmen and doing some homework online on sites that rate professors, you'll get a sense of direction here. There is some good information on sites like RateMyProfessor.com. You can learn a lot by looking at the range of comments about a specific professor, but don't blindly follow the opinions. Unless you know the students who have rated a specific professor, there are no guarantees that those reviews are accurate. Don't let your opinion be colored by one negative review. You don't know the rationale for the rating given and don't know if it's fair.

Also attempt to get some first-hand information. Students with the same or a similar major to yours who are further along in their programs *can* also be good information sources. They will have recently completed courses you need to take and have excellent "real life" experience with these professors. Key to mention is that you want to ask students who are doing well in their classes. Arguably, their advice is a bit more credible.

It can also be helpful to know that a professor often teaches a number of different classes within a field. He may teach Botany 201 (sophomore level class because it starts with a 2) *and* Botany 301 (a junior level class because it starts with a 3). If you like him for one (and do well), take him for another. It sounds simple, but it will be one less new teacher you will need to figure out in a given semester.

One last point about professors. Fame or authoring a book is not an effective measure of teaching ability. The skills required to engineer a breakthrough scientific finding, create a new financial theory or pen an amazing book are in fact very different from those required to effectively teach a class of 500. Even if the professor is highly acclaimed, before signing up for his course, ask some upperclassmen in your major what kind of experience they have had with him.

Picking the right professors can be a tremendous advantage in any major at any school.

Put it to work for you.

Taking a strategic approach
to selecting professors is always
an outstanding choice.

Listening Up

Barring any physical limitations, we can all listen, right? Wrong. We can all *hear*. A bit like seeing, hearing is not something we spend a whole lot of time working at. It just kind of happens. Not so with listening.

The ability (or lack of it) to truly listen and absorb information will have a major impact on your ability to excel in all aspects of your college experience and your career. It's also an important half of the **Communication Skills** equation — a half you'll definitely need to impress a grad school admissions panel or an employer.

It is quite interesting to think about the differences in the levels of training we receive in the areas of reading, writing, speaking, and listening. Of the four, we probably read or write the least. Between school, social and family conversation, TV, radio, movies, etc., we probably listen the most. Yet, we receive little or no training in listening skills. On the other hand, reading and writing are major parts of our educational system.

Listening should be active, not passive. To state the obvious, listening skills should be a focus area for you — particularly given that you'll spend more than 15 hours a week in college sitting in rooms *listening* to college professors. To do it well, you need the right environment and approach. Some specific steps you can take to maximize your effectiveness are as follows:

- Create proximity. Sit up front. While this is not a popular thought and has never been particularly "cool," it will definitely force you to be attentive. Even if the subject material that day is a bit on the "dry" side, common courtesy will keep you from snoozing if you're 10 to 15 feet from the lecturer. If you're in the last two or three rows, there's nothing to stop you from catching a few Z's and missing out on critical test material. Make it a habit to sit as close to the instructor as possible.

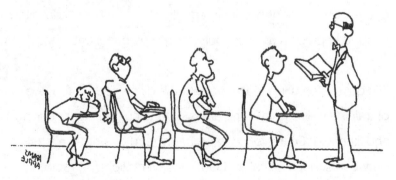

- Sit at attention. Lean forward. Don't slide back in your seat looking for the most comfortable position to settle in. Good, upright posture will help you mentally stay "in the game."

- Avoid distractions. Sit in a seat with a view of nothing interesting but the professor. Generally speaking, window (or window-view) seats are losing propositions. Too much interesting stuff to look at outside. Sitting up front also helps eliminate views of fellow classmates — who you also may find more interesting than the day's lecture material.

- Turn off unnecessary technology. Close all internet browsers on your computer — yes, that includes social networking sites. Shut down instant messaging. Close all programs other than a word processing program to take class notes. Shut down your e-mail. Dare I say it, I would even suggest you turn off your cell phone. When it starts vibrating every five minutes to let you know you have a new text message, the temptation to let yourself get distracted by reading them is great — and the temptation to respond to them is even greater. Bite the bullet. Turn it all off. If you're taking a class online, it will be somewhat impractical to turn off *all* your technology. You *will*, however, still want to turn off every possible distraction on your computer so you have one and only one option available to you — focusing on the task at hand.

- Focus intensely. Go in with the mentality that you're going to grasp and get notes on all key points made that day. Think about the subject matter and attempt to actually *understand* what the professor is telling you. Work at it.

- Put your laptop or pen to work. Make the effort to capture all new ideas and facts you are taught during the class. Many students can type faster than they can write, so laptops *can* be a great tool when used to aid your note-taking during class (if you're not distracted by advancing your social life).

- Ask questions. Nothing promotes poor listening like a fundamental lack of understanding.

One challenge in listening effectively is to fill what is called the "thought speed" gap. Simply put, you are able to process information a lot faster than the professor can deliver it.

In theory, you can think independently at a rate of more than 600 words per minute. A normal person will lecture at about 125 words per minute, leaving your mind a great deal of spare time to wander to anything but the subject at hand.

The thought speed gap doesn't necessarily mean you have to be bored. You can utilize this excess capacity to make sure you truly understand what the teacher is lecturing on and that your notes are meticulous. But, you have to work at it. If you catch yourself drifting, quickly refocus and get back in the game. Remember, we're making "listening" an *active* process. The more you practice this, the better you'll get at it.

And finally, plan to get a little mentally fatigued by the end of class. Active listening does take energy and will wear you down. The good news, though, is that it will have a major positive impact on your academic performance.

Active listening will enhance your retention of lecture material.

Notes-notes and Other Study Secrets

Studying is easy. It just takes time. Right? Studying *is* easy if your goal is just to *pass*. If you're looking for a B or better, a slightly more sophisticated approach is in order.

As I mentioned, the majority of professors lecture on the subject matter they believe is most important. It follows from this that they will test on those same areas. Let me repeat that. The majority of professors lecture on the subject matter they believe is most important. They will then test on the

subject matter from their lectures — to see if you have learned the information they thought was most important. Therefore, I can't overemphasize the importance of having *great* notes and knowing the material in them.

Let me explain what I mean when I say "know the material." Knowing means absorbing *and* understanding it, not just memorizing it. This is the major difference in college tests versus many you've had in high school. In high school, if you were able to memorize a list of things and write them down on the test, you were generally in pretty good shape. You didn't always have to know what the lists meant. You just needed to scribble them on paper. In college, if you don't truly understand the material, you'll get tripped up on the test. College exams are intentionally designed to reward thinkers and analyzers — people who can actually do something with information, not just memorize it. By the way, employers and grad schools reward the same skill sets.

I stumbled onto an interesting concept in high school that was the basis for a great deal of my academic success in college. My chemistry teacher, who was probably my best and most demanding high school teacher, covered a tremendous amount of material in his classes and expected us to know all of it — in great detail. As he flew through chapter after chapter, to increase our odds of survival, he let us bring a 3 x 5 index card into our tests with anything we wanted written on both sides of it. He actually encouraged us to bring "cheat sheets" to the test!

What I would do to prepare for these tests, of course, was skim my notes to try to figure out what was most important and most difficult in them. From there, I would transfer these points onto notebook paper and see if I had too much, too little, or just enough material to fit on my "cheat sheet." I always had too much information so I would have to pick out the most difficult and most important concepts from these condensed notes and then, with the finest point pen I could find, write them on my index card in the smallest type possible. I always took the index card into the test and set it out on my desk — but I never ended up looking at it. In the process of deciding what the most important and difficult concepts were, I accidentally learned them!

Hence the concept of "notes-notes."

Notes-notes could be the secret to your success.

Review your notes once thoroughly and make separate notes of the material that you think is most critical and was most emphasized in class. It will be things like key formulas, principles, key vocabulary, or lists of things. You'll find you'll be able to boil 50 to 60 pages of notes into five or six pages of true focus points. I call these new condensed notes your notes-notes. They are simply the notes from your notes. If you memorize them, understand them, and can apply them on your exam, you're well on your way to the grade you want.

Just using a highlighter on your old notes to create notes-notes in your notebook without doing any writing is *not* a good shortcut, and I'd strongly recommend against it. The exercise of writing the material down doesn't take that long and does actually help you learn the material. I won't bore you with brain function theory here, but the act of writing helps your brain engage and process the information. It really works!

When you start to study, spend time reviewing your notes-notes first. *Really* focus on them so that you "own" the content. When you do, you'll have mastered the fundamentals for success on the exam. After you've done that, *then* go back through your main notes and pick up the secondary points and details. Even if you run out of study time, you'll still be knowledgeable in the most critical areas. You'll be amazed at how far this will get you on a test.

Conversely, you can slowly plod through the notes, memorizing every word on every page with no emphasis or priorities. If you run out of time, you'll never grasp the big picture the professor is trying to teach you. You won't be able to reason your way to answers based on your understanding of those key points. You'll just be able to spit out what you memorized, and you'll get hammered on the test — a far inferior approach *and* result relative to using notes-notes.

Another outstanding reason for taking notes-notes (and keeping them after your exam) is that for cumulative finals you'll have a much easier time relearning the key lecture points from earlier in the semester. It's a lot more efficient to review 10 or 12 pages of notes-notes from previous tests than starting over with 150 pages of old notes to relearn. And, because the most important information from those test periods is in your notes-notes anyway, it's an excellent place to start. You'll have four or five finals in a one-week period, so this advantage can be *tremendous*.

One minor caveat here. If you bombed either of the two earlier tests during the semester/quarter, you need to determine whether you did a lousy job taking notes, making your notes-notes, or didn't learn the material captured in them. If you did a lousy job on the notes-notes, do them over. Notes-notes only help if you have the right material in your notes to start with and make good choices in terms of what to include in those notes-notes.

Other good things to include in your notes-notes are points that the professor strongly hints will be on the test. During class when he says something like "This is something that you would be well served not to forget," circle it, star it, and capitalize it. Some professors will clearly *tell* you that something will be covered on the test. They're not trying to "trick" you. They just think the piece of information or formula is so important that they want you to intensely study it and attempt to truly understand it.

Do whatever is necessary to highlight the focus point in your notes — but plan to put it in your notes-notes and plan to know it. I was always amazed at the number of people who would completely ignore the hints and do nothing to highlight their notes to make these points stand out. If the professor suggests that something may be on the test, there's a *very* strong chance it will be!

If the class is a numbers-based class (i.e., accounting, calculus, etc.) or any type of problem-solving class, rework the homework problems as a means of studying. Do not just look at the previous work you've done and review the thought process of solving them. Shut the book and do the problems from scratch. It's a more active form of studying and will lead to greater retention. Most problems you'll see on the test will have some similarity to homework problems you've previously been assigned. Truly understanding how to solve them will put you in a strong position on test day.

Get active and DO something!

Note that with both note review and problem-solving, I'm recommending an active approach rather than a passive one.

DO SOMETHING! Don't just rock on a library chair staring blindly at ink on a page.

You may know that a different approach than we've discussed here works best for you. Great! You're the one who needs to ace the test. But, some type of active *do something* approach is almost always the best choice.

I suppose I would be a bit remiss if I didn't mention textbooks in a chapter on studying. The politically incorrect reality is that you *may* be able to ignore them completely in some classes. If you can find out that test material will come only from the notes (and it will in many of your classes), you may be able to save yourself a whole lot of time and effort. On the other hand, some professors will ask you about things from your readings that weren't discussed in class. The real *key* is to learn how your professors test.

How will you know? You'll know one of two ways. First, you'll ask. There's nothing wrong with, on a one-on-one basis, asking a professor the question, "If I've taken excellent lecture notes and know everything in them, can I get an A on this test?" Professors will answer this question honestly, particularly if you ask it when 399 other people aren't listening. (They may answer a bit more "by the book" with the big group tuned in.) Regardless of their answers, follow their lead.

The other way you'll figure out that you can save some time and not read the textbook is your personal history with the teacher. If this is your second or third test in a class, it's not too tough to figure this out. You can also find out from friends who have previously had the professor for a class. This is much riskier, however, depending on the friend. Finally, you may have the same professor for different classes (like Economics 201 and 202). He will rarely use the assigned textbook for 202 if he ignored it during 201.

If you do need to focus on the book in addition to your notes, try to keep up with the reading on a week-to-week basis so you don't have 200 pages to read the week of the test. If you highlight the book as you read, you can just study your highlights. If you don't keep up (it's tough to keep up in *every* class), learn your notes-notes *before* getting into the book. They're usually more important anyway and the reading will go much faster and be more beneficial if you do. You'll already have a fundamental understanding of the material and will absorb many more of the details from the text.

One other way a textbook may come in handy is as an additional resource for clarification. Even if the professor is only testing from lecture material, the book can be a resource to eliminate confusion. If you just don't understand something the professor is saying (or can't get to her to ask a question), the book may explain it in a different way or offer an example that makes the concept easier for you to grasp.

Or, if you are a person who generally enjoys reading, go ahead and read the book for the additional perspective it will offer. But, if possible, know ahead of time if you *need* it to be successful.

I suppose I should also mention test files. If you can *legally* get your hands on tests the professor has given in the past, it *might* significantly help your effort. You'll get a feel for his style of testing and what material he thinks is important. Don't be your own worst enemy here though. Here are several examples of brilliant things I've seen done related to test files. To me, they seem like obvious "don'ts." But believe me, I've seen people try them and fail miserably. They are as follows:

- People spending the entire night before the test trying to run down a copy of last year's test rather than studying. Pure brilliance!
- People assuming that they have found the "holy grail" when they find the old test. Knowing that they will now *ace* the exam, they spend the night before the test at a party. Another fabulous idea!
- People not reading a question carefully on the test and assuming that it is exactly the same question as last year. They then answer it incorrectly, of course, and the professor smiles as he puts the "X" on your paper as he knows exactly what you just did. Way to go, Einstein!

Once again, professors, as a rule, are pretty bright, hard-working folks. Old tests will be helpful in giving you a feel for a professor's testing style but will *not* be identical to the tests you take and will *not* be your saving grace.

Another subject worth mentioning is studying with other people. Studying with other people *can* be very helpful and greatly improve your test results under the right conditions. As with most other things, though, there are do's and don'ts to consider if you're going to try it.

First, study with someone as smart or smarter than you are. You don't want to tutor someone the night before a test. It's extremely frustrating and leads to very poor results (for you, not them).

Second, make sure that both of you are prepared when you get together. It is most effective to learn the fundamentals on your own and use the joint study time to refine your knowledge and help each other with the fine points. If both people are not equally prepared (and have not been to class), you will either become a tutor again or you'll have to be rude and excuse yourself to go study alone. My suggestion in this case, by the way, would be to be rude and excuse yourself so you do well on the test. Someone else's lack of preparation is not your fault. They should have had the consideration to cancel your session if they weren't ready to contribute equally.

Third, do not study with someone for the first time the night before a huge test. Do it two or three nights before. That way, if it doesn't work out, you'll have time to rally and still do well on the exam.

Now that I've made studying with someone sound like a horror show, I will tell you that I had some great success with it. A guy asked me to study with him before a money and banking class (rough stuff). After I politely shared with him the multiple reasons why I couldn't study with him, he not so politely told me that he wasn't some parasite just looking to work from my notes, but that he had a 3.9 average and just thought we could cut our study time in half if we put two great brains together. I was impressed (and amused) enough by his brash attitude that I gave it a try. He and I studied together often for the rest of our college careers.

Again, finding a person to study with *can* be very helpful *if* you find the right person. By the way, this person needs to be someone you're comfortable enough with to tell her if the session is not helping you. When it happens, you need to be able to tell her that you want to study with her next time around, but that you need to go solo on that particular night. Remember, the goal is for this to work for *you* (and preferably *both* of you, obviously).

One other thought. Some departments have student tutors/mentors available for help in given subject areas. These services are often free. If you need extra help, try this, but remember there is generally a limited schedule for these tutors, and you will probably not be able to get one on short notice.

In closing, let me mention that hiring a tutor does not count as "studying with someone else." If you've used up your free opportunities, office hours and test prep sessions offered by the professor, a tutor can be incredibly helpful. Generally, tutors are knowledgeable and can assist you. But like anything else, there are good tutors and bad tutors. A *week* before a test is a great time to try a new tutor. The night before is not.

Study smart to succeed.

Power Studying: When to Do It

It's not enough to know *how* to study; you need to know *when* to study too. It may not be the difference between passing and failing, but it very well may be the difference between a C and an A or a B in a class. I offer several suggestions here.

Let's start with when *not* to study. The answer: all night. Pulling an "all nighter," literally staying up all night to study for a test, is nothing short of crazy.

At midnight, you drink a six pack of Diet Mountain Dew or down several Red Bulls and eat energy bars to help you stay awake. You're "Going For It!" As a result, you have a bit of a twitch and a glazed, wild-eyed look by about 2 a.m. By 4 a.m., the caffeine from the last couple of cans has kicked in and you're reading 14 pages a minute. You're comprehending literally nothing — but

The classic all nighter.

flying through the material! By 6 a.m., the caffeine is wearing off and you find your face falling into your notebook. By 8 a.m., you hit a brick wall. Your head is swimming. You're a little sick to your stomach (a big surprise), and you're so exhausted you hardly know what five plus five equals. It's now time to go take your test.

Gee, I wonder how you'll do?

Have you ever seen an athlete go through sleep deprivation the night before the big game? Does a politician stay up all night before his big debate? Does a CEO go sleepless before her annual meeting with the board of directors? Of course not. It would be ludicrous. How is an all nighter before a test any different? Simply put, it's not. It's *stupid*. It's *HIGHLY* self-destructive.

DON'T DO IT!

Get at least four hours of sleep the night before any test and you'll perform better on it. If you run out of study time, you may not get to review those final two chapters of the book. However, at least you'll remember your notes-notes, your original notes, and the six or seven chapters you *did* review.

After staying up all night, you'll likely remember *less* of everything you studied and your ability to reason your way to answers you're unsure of will be severely diminished. Remember, college tests are designed to make you think.

Also, remember to watch your caffeine. It can be an effective tool to help to keep you mentally focused if you're wearing down. But, just because *some* is good does not mean *more* is better. Too much caffeine will make you jittery and actually hurt your ability to concentrate. When you come back down off the ceiling in several hours, you'll realize that you've accomplished very little. Moderation is the key.

By the way, I do think many people lie about their study habits. They think they are *supposed* to pull all nighters — like it's some kind of badge of honor to be able to say that you

did. It's not *expected* or "cool" to pull an all nighter. It's stupid.

To avoid putting yourself in a position where your back is up against the wall, I'd recommend creating your notes-notes three or four days before an exam. You may not need to study three or four days for the test, but this first step will give you a good feel for how much material you need to know, how complex it is, and how well you currently know it.

If you have a question, you'll also be much more likely to be able to get to your professor, either in class or during office hours, to have it answered. If you wait until the day before a test to begin your effort, you have literally no chance of getting her help.

In general, though, what comes as a shock to even a lot of strong high school students, is that you will need to plan on studying a *LOT* more than you did in high school. There will be much, much more information to soak up as, generally speaking, you'll move more quickly through more complex material and take exams less frequently when you are in college. You'll also spend very little time in the class reviewing for the test. You're pretty much on your own.

There is no one-size-fits-all answer to the question of how much studying is enough. I have heard college freshmen say, "I studied three hours for that test and still got a C." My response is typically that I'm not surprised. Think in terms of seven or eight *HOURS*... maybe 10–12 hours for a test in a class that is more difficult and carries more credit hours (and, therefore, has a bigger impact on your GPA). Really.

But remember, every class is different and so is every student. Just start early and keep working at it until you feel like you have a good grasp of the subject matter. You'll know when you're ready.

When during the day to study is another consideration. As I mentioned earlier, I'm a big believer in studying *between* classes. Unfortunately, just studying between classes won't be enough to prepare for a big test or finals. Because of that, you need to figure out what *part* of the day is the most effective study time for you. Some people are morning people. Some people are night people. Study during the part of the day when you are most alert and most productive. It sounds simple enough, but a lot of people don't do it. It's much trendier to be able to say you stayed up until 4 a.m. studying than to say that you got up

at 6 a.m. to hit the books. For many students, however, they're more effective studiers at 6 a.m.

How many beers to have before studying is another decision point. You know the answer, so I won't have to sound like your mom or dad again by telling you. When you're working, work. When you're having fun, have fun. Mixing the two is not really that much fun and it's not at all effective.

Studying at optimal times will make a difference. Take advantage of them and help separate yourself from the pack.

Power Studying: Where to Do It

Also under the subject of "sounds simple enough," you need to study in the right environment. Study in a quiet place where there will be no interruptions. You could study eight hours in front of the TV or two hours in the corner of the top floor of the library, and you'll most likely do better in the latter case. And realistically speaking, you weren't having that much fun in front of the TV with your sociology notes in your lap.

An *uncrowded* corner of the library is a good choice, or any truly remote place you can find. Key here is to make your study time as productive as you can. That way you'll need less of it. Three horrible places to study are 1) with chatty friends, 2) in a fraternity or sorority house, and 3) in a part of the library with lots of walk-by traffic. All of these would be more enjoyable than a boring, quiet study spot, but you'll get nothing done from an

Studying at its lowest level.

academic standpoint and won't have as much fun as you would have had if you were fully focused on having fun during that period of time. Poor time management.

Let me elaborate on the area of the library with lots of walk-by traffic — the "social section." If you go to the library and park yourself in the social section, you will severely damage your odds of success on the upcoming exam. Hey, I think the social section is great. You won't find a better place for conversation or to meet a date for next Saturday night. There is an opportunity in every other seat. Just don't study there!

I've also heard the social section referred to as "turtle row." Every time people hear footsteps, every head pops up to see who's walking by. Go watch it some time. It's actually kind of amusing.

If you really, really want to be in the social section, you can use a 15-minute trip there as a reward for two hours of intensive effort in the corner of the library basement. A visit can be a bit of an incentive to help you produce good, lengthy stretches of quality study time. The short visit will also make you feel good about the study progress you are making relative to your classmates.

One other bad place to study is within 100 miles of other people who are taking the same class and are less prepared than you are. *RUN* from them. *HIDE* from them. Do *anything* you can to stop them from getting to you. They'll want to ask you lots of questions, borrow your notes to copy them, or just talk for 15 minutes about how tough the class is and how unprepared they are. Avoid this whole ordeal. Find a quiet, out-of-the-way place and you won't have to either, 1) waste your time, or 2) apologize to them that you can't help them or chat about life.

One quiet study location that can be good or bad, depending on the individual, is in bed. If the room is quiet, some people can intensely focus in this comfortable setting. Under the same conditions, others will fall asleep in 10 minutes or less. If you're going to try this one, don't do it when you're tired or the night before a big test. Try it several nights before and see how it works.

If you follow the advice in this section, you'll not only improve your academic performance, you'll have more free time to pursue other more enjoyable endeavors, however you may define them. You may even want to grab a miscellaneous textbook, go to the social section of the library, and try to get a date for Saturday night.

> You won't be hurting any other student's chance of success by talking to them in the "social section" of the library. They're not getting anything done anyway!

Taking Tests

Before I tackle the topic of effective test taking, I'll let you know that I'm going to make the assumption that you've studied adequately before the test. If you haven't studied, you're dead. *It's that simple.* The techniques I'll share with you will give you an extra edge, not resurrect you from the dead. Sorry.

If you don't study, you're dead.

The methods I'll share do work well. However, if you had straight A's in high school, don't completely abandon your old test taking techniques. They seem to be working well for you so far!

Okay, here we go. When you first get the exam, take two minutes and scan the whole test. Will you be pressured for time or will you have time to really think through and answer every question? Will it be a bear or a breeze? Obviously, the tests that are both lengthy and difficult are the most troublesome. Regardless, know what you're up against *immediately*.

After looking over the test, if it looks long or tough, don't panic. Just start knocking it out — one question at a time. Sitting in shock for 15 minutes will not help the situation! Start *simple* — go to the questions you're sure you can answer correctly. This will do two things. First, you'll pick up the easy points. If you run out of time, you'll have skipped the difficult questions rather than the "gimmes." Second, you'll generate some positive momentum for yourself.

Once you know you've picked up 35 or 40 of a possible 100 points in the first 10 minutes, you'll be calmer and more confident. You'll be panicky and feel rushed if you start by attempting to take on the toughest questions first.

Next, move to remaining high value questions, the ones worth the most points. You'll want to have time to give these some quality thought. Remember, how long it takes to answer a question is not always consistent with how much it's worth.

If the values are not spelled out, the simplest, best approach is to hit the "gimmes" first, then go from top to bottom. Just don't spend too much time thinking about a question that has you stumped. You can come back to it at the end of the test if time permits. And, sometimes another question will trigger a thought that will help you solve the question that looked like a stumper when you first saw it.

If the test is multiple-choice, a strategic approach to the test can make a tremendous difference in your results. After you read each question, try to answer it mentally before you read the options presented as answers. This will allow you to potentially crystallize your thoughts before being confused by potential *trick* answers. Next, read all the answers to ensure that your initial answer was the right choice. If you draw a blank, think of the question as multiple *elimination*. Read the answers, immediately eliminating the choices that you know aren't correct.

On most tests, there are usually only two reasonable answers to a question. By using the elimination process, you've got a 50% chance of getting the question right even if you haven't got a clue.

One final point on multiple-choice tests. If you need to transfer your answers onto a separate answer sheet, be *VERY* careful to match the question number on the test to the question number on the answer sheet. Double or triple check this. If you're off by just one answer (you answer question #8 in the #9 spot on the answer sheet), it will get *VERY* ugly from there as you'll miss every subsequent question.

On an essay test, the rules change completely. The objective here is to download every possible thing in your brain related to the subject onto the piece of paper. No points are awarded for impressive sentence structure (unless it's an English class). Just get the information onto the page. And, unless you are told differently, on an essay test, you get no extra points for being brief and "to the point."

In grading an essay test, a professor is looking for your answer to provide specific information. For each "nugget" she finds, you get points. Key vocabulary words and catch phrases will be critical to you. Use them wherever and whenever you can work them in. When grading 400 handwritten tests, the professor (or her assistant) can get tired. In that case, the vocabulary words and catch phrases can add many valuable points to your test score.

Obviously, the essay test favors the individual with a full mind and a fast pen. Don't waste time, *BUT*, think through your answer *before* putting pen to paper.

Take the time to organize your thoughts and jot down a few notes. *THEN*, put your head down and don't stop writing until the bell rings and the class is over. One almost painfully obvious point related to this is that your writing must be legible. The mood of any person grading literally hundreds of tests can go sour in a hurry when she has to spend extra time deciphering your scribbling.

If you don't understand a question on a test, ask the professor to rephrase it for you. You won't be able to do this in every situation, and, some professors won't answer a question during a test. In other situations, the teacher's assistant (TA) is giving the test for the professor and may or may not be able to help. But, you've got nothing to lose by asking, and in many cases it will be the difference between getting the answer right or wrong. An additional reason to ask the question is that professors may

*A really
bad idea.*

inadvertently give you clues to the correct answer in attempting
to clarify the question for you.

Another key point on test taking — *DON'T CHEAT*. I know I sound
like I'm preaching again, but I've seen people try it in college and
get caught. It's ugly. Even if cheat sheets were your bread and
butter in high school, let me bluntly tell you that the stakes here
are significantly higher, so you'll need to change your approach.

If you're caught, in a best-case scenario, you'll get a zero for
the test or may get kicked out of the class. The F will go onto
your transcripts and will seriously damage your GPA. And,
you're probably going to have to explain it to someone (like a
prospective employer) somewhere down the line. If you're less

fortunate, you'll be put on probation or kicked out of school.

Said another way, colleges take cheating *SERIOUSLY*. If you get caught, you're fried. It's just not worth it. I could also spend paragraphs on the fact that even if you don't get caught, it's wrong. But, I'm hoping that I have adequately spelled out the potential consequences of crossing the line and, therefore, I have effectively dissuaded you!

One final thought on test-taking. You may be able to pick up some additional points *after* taking the test if you've already developed a strong relationship with your professor. Go see her and politely talk to her about any points of disagreement you have on how she graded your test. If you thought a multiple-choice question had two correct answers, make your case as to why your answer was *also* correct. Make the case respectfully, but make sure she understands your thought process and why you believe you deserve the credit. If you think she misunderstood your essay answer, it is *definitely* worth a discussion. Be prepared, do it professionally and with a cool head, and sometimes you can pick up some critical points — *if* you have laid the groundwork *beforehand* and have a good relationship with her.

> There's no need to panic about test-taking if you're properly prepared.

Finals Week(s)

College tests can be tough. In classes in your major or those designed to weed out people who want to get into a popular or competitive major, they're even tougher. Even with the study and test taking skills you've learned thus far, you'll need a winning study strategy and a meaningful time commitment to do well on *one* test.

Finals are a *MUCH* bigger challenge than a single typical college-level test. Most finals will be *cumulative*, covering not just six or eight weeks of material, but the information covered in an entire semester (or quarter). Sometimes a final can be worth 50% or more of the grade for the term. And, just to make it interesting, you'll have to take between four and six finals during the *same week*, probably all between Monday and Thursday. Welcome to Finals Week.

In a matter of 100 hours or so, your GPA for the term could go from a 3.0 to a 4.0. It might also go to a 2.0. Words like "challenging" and "stressful" do not begin to explain what you'll be up against.

To say that nothing you have previously experienced in your academic life has prepared you for this *battle* would be accurate... perhaps even a bit of an understatement, but accurate nonetheless.

Do I have your attention?

I hope so.

Done right, finals week can be a *tremendous* opportunity to make a semester of intelligent study habits pay off with a strong final surge to your GPA. Done poorly, well, let's not talk about that.

Let's talk about how to make finals week *work* for you.

First, think about the experience as finals *WEEKS*. It's *not* finals week. It's a two-week process that starts the Monday before you take your first test. Really.

Second, determine how much studying you'll need to do. Make an educated guess as to how many hours you'll need to study for each specific test. If you've been to class, have the notes, have the notes-notes, and have done the reading that was absolutely necessary, I would guess that you'll need 12–15 hours per class. That's right, not 12–15 hours *overall,* 12-15 hours *per* class. This will obviously vary by individual and by class, but it's not a bad starting point.

If you think I've lost my mind (you probably do), let's take a step back and look at what's at stake. After five semesters of finals, you'll be looking for an internship. Not after eight semesters — after five. If you want to try to get one between your sophomore and junior years (see the "Internships" section), now you're talking *three* semesters. Your internship(s) (or lack of them) will have a significant impact on the full-time job you'll get.

You'll need a strong GPA to be considered for quality internships and jobs. And, because how you fare on finals will have more impact on your GPA than any other single thing, there's no better time to step up and go above and beyond than during finals *weeks*. *EVERYONE* on campus will study non-stop during finals week. By studying incredibly hard the week *before* finals, you'll set yourself apart from almost all other students. One week for each of those five (or three) semesters will fundamentally impact your future. This commitment is a *VERY* small price to pay for future greatness.

So, in planning your finals studying process effectively, you'll know how many hours you'll need to spend in total to be prepared to do well on all your tests. Determining this on the Sunday *eight days before finals start* will give you the opportunity to make the necessary time commitment to get the job done right.

From here, based on your class-by-class study needs, make a day-to-day, hour-by-hour, class-by-class schedule and *STICK TO IT*. Include things on the schedule like going to class, eating, sleeping, doing laundry, etc. You will need to do these things. Add any study sessions your professors are offering. Then, fill in the schedule with your proposed study time by subject area (i.e., Tuesday 1-4 p.m. calculus).

You'll find when you make your schedule that if you have no tests on Thursday and only one on Friday, you may be able to do all your studying for that Friday test after you are done with the others on Wednesday. Because of this, make your study schedule *starting with your last test first* and work your way back in reverse order from there. This will leave you with the most logical study schedule for the two-week period and will ensure you don't run out of time to study for your last tests (a common problem for non-planners during finals week).

You should also plan to study for a given final the last couple of hours before you go take that test (versus studying for another exam). It will get you focused, build your confidence, and keep the material in your short-term memory. Believe me, you'll need it.

You may find when you put together this schedule that you'll have virtually no time to do much else in the next 10 days. If that's the case, keep remembering what's at stake. You know what your priority needs to be! You may also find that you have some time each day in the first week for a good study break... be it a movie, a game of basketball, or a trip to Subway or Starbucks. That's great.

You will clearly, however, know what you'll need to do to get the job done. You'll also know that you'll have some time off *after* finals to catch your breath. You'll need it!

A couple of other points.

Don't make the experience a two-week sleep deprivation experiment. Your body can't perform well in that scenario. Make sure you're getting at least six hours of sleep per night in week one and at least four hours per night during the actual finals week. This may vary. Know your own body and make intelligent decisions.

One piece of good news here is that you'll also have a bit more study time during finals week than during a typical week. Why? Because you don't have classes during finals week. Lots of places also have *"dead days."* These aren't days to recover from a party life that has nearly killed you. They are days designed to allow you extra time to prepare for those grueling finals you'll have to take. They will provide you with some extra quality hours that you'll probably desperately need at that point in time.

Of course, the other key to success is to stay *calm*. If your study schedule is realistic and you follow it, you'll be fine. Freaking out will not assist you in the process in any way.

Just keep a cool head and put in the necessary time.

Think about finals week as finals weeks. Start early and you'll be surprised at how well you'll do.

CHAPTER 6
The Winning Edge: Extracurriculars

You've got the grades. You've got the big interview. You're so close to getting your dream job that you can *taste* it. You SEE yourself in that job!

You go into the interview and get *BOMBARDED* with questions — almost none of which relate to your outstanding GPA. The recruiter wants concrete examples of when you exhibited **Leadership** to make an organization truly better, of when you showed **Entrepreneurship** to change the status quo, of how you used **Logic** to get out of a tough jam, and of when you showed **Communication** and **Group Skills** in working with others.

> Virtually **any organization can provide an opportunity** to build your resume.

Are you rock solid or collapsing under the barrage of questions?

If you haven't been heavily involved in extracurricular activities, you're going to crumble. You have no answers, and you have no job. So, how do you pass *this* test with flying colors?

Let's take a look.

Virtually any organization can provide you with an opportunity to build your resume.

There's no one magic club, honorary, or other extracurricular activity that every employer is seeking. It's your track record in the organization, not the title of the group, or for that matter the number of groups, that makes the difference. So make the **Effort** and get involved in something you think you'll enjoy and be good at. It can be anything from student government to a meaningful club, community service organization or a sorority. And, if you get involved in numerous groups and keep your grades up, you will strongly demonstrate your **Organizational Skills**. It's up to you to choose what to pursue. Just get involved! I'll explain in the next chapter what to do *after* you join — but just getting involved is a good first step.

REMEMBER if you don't have a strong extracurricular record, your interviews will most likely be filled with silence or shallow conversation. Your GPA will *get* you the interview. You won't get a good look without strong grades.

But, unless you're strong in activities or have incredible work experience (we'll talk about that later), you'll have nothing to talk about other than your GPA.

You won't be able to *prove* that you have the **Winning Characteristics**.

If you can't **prove you have the** Winning Characteristics, someone else will get your dream job.

Making Your Mark

Making significant differences in organizations or in a workplace setting during college is not a nice extra — it's a must. I *CANNOT* emphasize that point enough.

Focusing for now on non-work experiences, you can make your mark through organizations related to your field of study, student government, the fraternity/sorority system, charitable groups, community involvement, or in a variety of other ways. I know of no better way to *prove* that you have the **Winning Characteristics** than by pursuing extracurricular activities.

Let me clarify what I mean by "making your mark" or "making significant differences." This is important. Boiling it down, a group needs to be meaningfully different and better because *YOU* were a part of it. Another way to think about it would be to ask yourself the question, "What good things would not have happened if you were not a part of the group?" It's not about what title you held or how popular the group was on your campus. It's about what you were able to actually accomplish as a part of the group. I cannot stress this enough. (See **Leadership** in the section about the **Winning Characteristics**)

Okay, so how do you make your mark?

It doesn't happen overnight. You have to first join an organization and commit enough time to understand it in detail. As you grasp the fundamentals, think about how you can make it better. Or, looking at it from a slightly different angle, try to figure out what is stopping the organization from being as good as it can possibly be. Ask current and past leaders of the group what they think the key opportunities are. Talk to any other relevant people on campus to get their perspectives.

As a road map, think about the following questions. How can the organization be *bigger, broader reaching, better funded*, or *more effective* in achieving its core mission? After doing some research and giving it some thought, you should be able to develop some initial thoughts as to how you're going to make your mark. Get input on those from key stakeholders — officers, the faculty advisor, or other appropriate individuals — to confirm you're on the right track.

From there, you'll need to convince the group that your idea is the right thing to do, get them to rally behind you, and make your idea(s) a reality. You may have to start small to prove that your ideas are good and that you're committed enough to pull them off.

However, once you build credibility, the sky is the limit! You could even end up running the group. From there, you can *really* make things happen.

If at all possible, it's very helpful if you can somehow prove the organization was tangibly better from your efforts (i.e., more members, better financial position, better programs). What metrics/measurements can you use to objectively support your case? This type of ammunition is your ticket to the dream job in an interview situation.

See, making your mark is simple. Okay, it's not simple, but it is incredibly *IMPORTANT*.

As you think about how you might do this, it's important that you know that you do not have to accomplish show-stopping, dramatic, Guinness Book of World Records type things in making your mark. You just need to make some positive differences. Let me give you a few examples from my college experience.

I joined a fraternity at Miami. I never planned to get involved in the Greek system, but because it was the center of the school's social activity — and I definitely wanted a social life — it made sense. After I joined a very small fraternity, primarily because I liked the people, I saw an opportunity to help improve the struggling organization and got heavily involved.

I became social chairman during my sophomore year and threw some great parties that were well attended and that helped build our reputation on campus. During junior year, I was elected president and set out to significantly improve the fraternity for the long term. Working with the other elected officers, I came up with some new ideas and generated support for them with our members (**Leadership**, **Organization**, **Entrepreneurship**, **Communication**, etc.).

For instance, we tightened up our standards and changed the criteria for membership in the organization. No longer would someone be allowed to become a member simply because he was a "good guy," we had room for him in the house, and needed the money he would pay for room and board. Applicants would have to show a pursuit of excellence in some aspect of their college life — scholastically, socially, athletically — or in some other way to join the organization.

If the group was going to be as strong as it could be, we needed individuals representing the fraternity to be leaders on campus.

Thinking **Logically**, we decided that if we wanted to *attract* quality, we had to *show* quality.

This was a tough financial decision. We had to tighten our belt the first year when we limited admission to eight pledges (versus a typical class of 20). It paid off in the second year in the quality and number of people who joined, and the fraternity has been more successful ever since. Within 10 years, it had doubled in size and had become one of the strongest on campus.

You can make your mark in a wide variety of ways. An unorthodox but meaningful example of how I made my mark was my effort related to a tug-of-war event on campus. It was an annual competition among all of the 24 fraternities. Okay, it was a bit silly, but half of the campus, about 5,000 people, would come out to watch us grunt a lot, get muddy, tear up our hands, and try desperately to win this silly but high-profile event.

We decided that if we wanted to be seen as a major fraternity on campus, we could help build our reputation if we could do well in this popular event. By the way, my fraternity was usually blown out in the first round of this event. Showing **Leadership**, I helped organize our team and developed a new pulling technique that allowed our small but athletic team to compete against some of the horses we would be up against. I didn't do it alone — but I was a key driver of the effort — which is all you really need to be. From there, for two weeks, we practiced every night after dinner.

You can make an impact in any number of ways.

This was no small task as we had to convince 15 additional guys from the fraternity to come out and pull against the 10 of us who would represent our organization in the event. Needless to say, they all had lots of other options as to how they could spend that time.

We beat one of the biggest fraternities on campus and came in fifth place out of 24 teams. Not bad for a very small fraternity. In our second year, we beat the defending champs and came in second place, receiving a standing ovation from the huge crowd (and achieving our goal of improving our image on campus).

This obviously wasn't rocket science. In fact, it was a tremendous amount of fun. We had a blast. *AND*, it gave me a story that allowed me to show recruiters that I was **Entrepreneurial** enough to come up with a way to use a simple sporting event as a way to build our image, had enough **Logic** to help create an innovative pulling technique that leveraged our strength and mitigated our lack of bulk, had the **Group Skills** to get 25 guys to actively participate, and was willing to put forth the **Effort** to pull it off. And, we were successful in achieving our goal.

It's exactly the kind of stuff grad schools and recruiters are looking for!

An example more directly related to my future career was a marketing program I put together for a local restaurant during my senior year. I did it as a part of my involvement in a marketing group, Pi Sigma Epsilon. I joined the group because I knew I could use more experience in the marketing area, and they were the strongest marketing organization on campus.

A restaurant owner called us for some free advice on how he could improve his business. It was not a high priority project for the group, so I had the opportunity, even as a rookie, to step in as a newer member and **Lead** it. After doing some research, we developed a comprehensive proposal on how we thought the owner could improve his business. He successfully used some of the ideas. The business became more profitable, and I had another positive story of how I had exhibited the **Winning Characteristics** to share during interviews.

Another area loaded with opportunities to make your mark is community service. This type of involvement can be impressive on a resume and is a legitimate way for you to go out and do a little bit of good in the world. An **Entrepreneurial** example here could be setting up a successful student Red Cross blood drive or local United Way campaign that had not been previously undertaken — or the significant improvement of one already in place. You'd be amazed at the reaction that a successful program of this type would generate.

Many businesses have strongly increased their focus on giving back to the community. Some even have formal programs allowing employees to do service work during work hours. Given that, they are very tuned in to service and may respond well to your service-oriented stories.

Today's professionals in all fields want their organizations to be seen as positive contributing members of their local communities. If they think you can help with this, it could give you an edge.

Here's an important clarification, however. Focus on *quality*, not *quantity* in your resume building process. Making a significant contribution to two or three groups is much more meaningful than being a weak, non-contributing member of 17 different groups.

Remember, unless you *DO* something meaningful in organizations you join, you still have *NOTHING* to talk about on interview day.

As you think about what you'll pursue, don't focus on only *one* organization. If you don't get elected to a key position or things don't work out for one reason or another, you'll want to have some other options available. This point is critical as you'll be competing with other strong students for the best roles in these groups. You'll want to give yourself several opportunities to "win" in different organizations.

Also, the organizations don't have to be the most popular ones on campus. Whether an organization is *the* group on campus or a smaller, lower profile one isn't terribly relevant. Recruiters care much more about what you did to improve, change, or build the group for the better than they do about which organizations they were. Again, they're simply looking for evidence of the **Winning Characteristics**.

A key element of being able to make your mark in *any* group is to start early. *DON'T WAIT TO BE GREAT!* If you want to prove yourself, get elected to a key office, and perform at a high level to make a real difference, you'll need to be in that group for two or three years. That means you should start, at the *latest*, at the beginning of your sophomore year.

One other important consideration is whether or not you should start your own student organization. Really! Definitely consider starting your own group if you see an opportunity to do so. Creating something from nothing is a great challenge and will impressively display your skills in all of the **Winning Characteristics**.

As an example, if you love to ride horses and your school doesn't have an equestrian club, why not start one? If you're interested in the stock market and there's no investment club, creating one is a great opportunity. You'll most likely have to work through the school's student activities department to formally be recognized as a campus organization. However, schools want to be able to market the fact that they have a large and growing number of student organizations, so they will most likely be very supportive if they feel that your new group fills an unmet need.

One final benefit of starting your own organization is that you don't need to get elected to hold office. You're the founder and president! It takes the risk of not getting *elected* out of the equation. Also, being a co-founder or co-president is just as impressive as founding it alone — so find a friend with similar interests to pursue the adventure with you.

Individual activities (non-group opportunities) can also be a plus. I tutored students in economics during my junior and senior years. I didn't spend a tremendous amount of time doing it, but it suggested to recruiters that I was at least relatively intelligent (**Logic**) and could **Communicate** with others. As a part of an overall record of achievement, small activities and accomplishments can make a difference.

And remember, it's important to get involved in something that is truly of interest to you. You're going to put in some major time and **Effort**, and you'll work harder and perform better if you care about what you're doing. If you aren't truly committed, your effort won't be consistent; it will be obvious to your fellow members, and you won't have much hope of being a leader or making much of a difference.

Get involved or get left behind
in your future job hunt.

Clubs and Honoraries

Clubs and honoraries are a real mixed bag. They can be extremely helpful or a complete waste of time and money. The right ones can open doors for you. The wrong ones are no more than a way to spend $75, get a pin that you'll never wear again, and put some Greek letters on your resume.

The definition of an "honorary" versus a "club" can vary greatly by organization and by school. Typically, an honorary is a group that offers you an invitation to join based on some type of achievement (e.g., good grades or service). Some honoraries, like any activity, also provide excellent networking opportunities.

A club will grant membership for an endless number of reasons depending on the type of group it is and how exclusive it's attempting to be.

A specific club or honorary can be a great opportunity or a complete waste of time. You'll need to "scratch below the surface" before joining to see if a specific group is worth your time (and money).

Good ones offer outstanding opportunities for you to exhibit the **Winning Characteristics** if you take **Leadership** positions in them and make good things happen as a result of your personal efforts.

As I mentioned, I was a member of a marketing club called Pi Sigma Epsilon my junior and senior years and helped a restaurant with its marketing. Big deal, right? While some recruiters hadn't heard of PSE, it gave me an accomplishment to talk about in my interviews. It's a terrific example of the fact that an action-oriented group will take you a lot farther than one that has a fancy name (or reputation on campus) and gives you a pin to put in your drawer. It also demonstrates that *what* you do in an organization is more important than which one you do it in.

Clubs and honoraries related to your major are generally a good opportunity. If you haven't already done so, stop by the department office for your major to find out what's available and what the criteria are to join each group.

These organizations will help educate you on the range of jobs available in your field. They'll also introduce you to potential internship opportunities, future employers, and give you opportunities to begin to build important relationships well before your first interview. If you can use them as a way to demonstrate the **Winning Characteristics**, all the better.

The accounting honorary I was a member of, Beta Alpha Psi, held monthly receptions hosted by large accounting firms that interviewed at our school. These events gave me great opportunities to meet some important people in the industry and find out what each firm had to offer in terms of types of jobs, salaries, working environment, and potential for advancement. The receptions also gave me a chance to learn how to

You get what you earn.

successfully carry on conversations with business professionals who were twice my age. This didn't come naturally to me, but it got easier with practice and I was very comfortable talking to recruiters within six months — well before any interviews actually started.

There was one more tremendous benefit to going to these receptions. I found that when I went to interview, I had already met some of the recruiters. This immediately lowered my stress level and helped me perform well in the interviews. And, by the way, an extra bonus to the receptions is that they have free food there — and it's usually pretty good.

Key to mention, though, is that the best (and most helpful) honoraries are not typically open to all students. You need strong grades and/or an impressive record of service to be invited to join.

Fraternities and sororities are a whole different kind of "club." As I mentioned, I never thought I would join a fraternity. I ended up doing so on a whim, and it turned out to be one of the best decisions I made in college. Fraternities and sororities are loaded with opportunities for you to build and exhibit the **Winning Characteristics**. They tend to have five or so elected officers and another 10 to 15 positions of responsibility in the organization. If the group has a house that students live in, there are even more opportunities to take on a position of responsibility within the group. Each role is an opportunity to learn and strengthen your resume.

But, beware. Almost every fraternity and sorority has a group of hard-core "party people" who have a great time *but* slide through with C averages. They present a 24/7 opportunity to party… literally. They're a lot of fun but don't seem to have nearly as good a time living back at home waiting tables for a living after college. There's nothing wrong with waiting tables, but you don't need a college degree (or college loans to pay) to do it.

There are many ways to get involved and make a real contribution with any *legitimate* club or honorary. With elected and appointed positions, you can always find a way to make an *impact* at some level. If you do a good job, the opportunities will grow from there. Those opportunities will be whatever you make of them.

On a less positive note, I have found no value whatsoever in paying $75 to be in something like the Sophomore Scholastic Honorary if it never meets and has no active role on campus or in the community. A recruiter will care less. Or worse yet, because you thought it was meaningful enough to be included on your resume, they'll ask you about your involvement in and contribution to the group. Good luck answering that question!

I feel the same way about the "Who's Who" books. You get your name in a big book with literally thousands of other people who are also supposedly "special," and you all get the opportunity to buy the book to collect dust on your book shelf for $50. Awfully impressive, isn't it?

Clubs and honoraries *can* be of real benefit. Let me restate that. They can be of real benefit *if* you take the time and effort to make a true impact — to once again exhibit that you have the **Winning Characteristics**. On the other hand, for most any organization you're part of, if belonging to it only means getting your name on a list and going to an induction ceremony, it probably isn't worth your time.

Get involved. Just stay away from the worthless, resume filler stuff.

Organized Sports

Does anybody really care if you're the second string center fielder on your college baseball team?

Well, actually, they do.

There are some real positives to being involved in athletics at the intercollegiate or club level (or even the intramural level).

Athletic participation shows you are willing to put forth tremendous **Effort** to succeed. To do well, you have to be self-disciplined enough to keep working at it. You can't be a quitter. Recruiters like that. In fact, there are companies that specifically target NCAA athletes because they know how hard it is to be a student-athlete these days and know that an individual who can keep a good GPA and successfully compete at the college level has a pretty amazing work ethic. Their theory, drawn from behavioral-based interviewing, is that this work ethic will translate to their company after college.

Most sports allow you to exhibit your **Group Skills** by being a contributing team player. This includes things like making personal sacrifices for the good of the group. It involves cooperating with fellow team members who aren't necessarily your best friends.

Being involved in sports is another way to develop and demonstrate **Communication Skills**. It's tough to be effective on a high-level team without them.

Participation in competitive intercollegiate sports gives you a chance to show that you possess **Logic**. Most sports at the college level involve strategy and require you to be able to think well under pressure to succeed. You need a lot more than to be able to throw or catch a football well to excel in NCAA sports. The days of recruiters viewing athletes as "dumb jocks" are a thing of the past.

It also takes some strong **Organizational Skills** to effectively manage a full college course load and the day-to-day requirements of college-level sports. College sports take up a great deal of time, forcing you to be highly organized to even survive your classes, much less maintain a good grade point average.

For intercollegiate sports, in season, you can plan on a commitment of two to six hours per day — every day. Big school or small, they take their athletics *very* seriously. At a lot of places, playing for the school team is like having a full-time job. And, most sports have home and away events. When you have away games or matches, it will be an even bigger time commitment, sometimes taking up a full day or even an entire weekend. And, don't count on a whole lot of sympathy from your professors. Even if you're the next international sports icon, you won't get much "charity" from your professors at most schools. You'll be expected to get the work done like any other student.

You'll need to be priority-focused and a good time manager to keep your grades up during the peak periods of the season. You may even consider scheduling your most difficult classes around your athletics. Take a heavier load, if possible, during the off-season.

If you're a very good athlete but not able to compete at the NCAA level, club sports may also be an option to consider. Club sports are generally well organized and share many of the characteristics of traditional intercollegiate athletics. You'll practice, have an official schedule, and compete against different schools. The quality of the competition will still be quite good and the time commitment will still be significant. But, club sports can be a great deal of fun and *may* allow you to exhibit the **Winning Characteristics** in the same way as NCAA sports if you make that a focus. It's all about how you approach the activity and your accomplishments along the way.

Finally, on a level that most of us can relate to, even participation on your residence hall's intramural softball team will help you in your job pursuit. Along with allowing you to show you are a good team player (among other things), it will allow you the chance to relax, take a break from your busy schedule, and get in a little exercise.

And, who knows, the company you're interviewing with may need a good shortstop for its employee softball team.

> So, don't overlook organized sports
> as a way to set yourself apart.

Personal Fitness

Participation in intramural sports, or any other sports-related activity, offers one more important benefit. It keeps you physically fit.

As I once again step into the land of the politically incorrect, let me state that recruiters like candidates who look like they make an attempt to take care of themselves. If you ever asked a recruiter if that were the case, she would absolutely deny it. From a legal standpoint, she *has to* deny it or she will open her company up to a discrimination lawsuit.

Fortunately, recruiters aren't looking for body builders or beauty queens. They don't care if you're tall or short, or have a large or small frame. Fifteen percent body fat or less is *not* a requirement to be hired by any firm. But, you can help your cause by creating a first impression that gives a recruiter the sense that you make an effort to take care of your body.

Is this fair?

No.

Is it real?

Yes.

Could you ever prove that you were discriminated against on the basis of size/weight? Probably not. The recruiter may not even know that he or she is doing it — she just "likes" one candidate better than the other.

Are physically fit people more energetic and motivated than people who are out of shape? Do they have more discipline and self-control and therefore make better employees? Who knows! Every person is different. But, if you'll make a better impression if you're physically fit, isn't it worth the effort? This *is* your career and your future we're talking about.

Someone who exercises regularly is also a better risk to a company from a health standpoint. This is also of interest to some employers. In fact, many companies build fitness centers for their employees to encourage them to work out (thereby cutting future company medical costs). Other organizations will reimburse their staff for membership in a local fitness club. Fitness is well beyond being a "craze." It's here to stay.

Let me suggest that you actually *schedule* fitness into your week. If you build it into your day and put it into your planner like a class or a meeting, you'll be a lot more likely to actually get to the fitness center. You won't schedule another meeting during a time frame when you had planned to workout. You won't forget. And, when you put something in writing, it feels like more of a commitment so you're more likely to get it done. Finally, to state the obvious, if you're slammed and not ready for a big test tomorrow, skip the workout scheduled in your planner and hit the library. Work out after the test.

Remember, you *don't* need to be a bodybuilder to impress an employer.

Just get and stay in shape and you may have a leg up on interview day.

Expanding Your World

There's a whole world out there… and you ought to know at least a *little* bit about it.

You don't need to become obsessed with world events, but you should dedicate at least a couple of hours each week to understanding what's going on in the world (and in your desired profession). Make the effort to expand your world with some outside reading, targeted web surfing, or news-oriented TV shows. The process may be a little painful at first as you may not understand what you're reading/seeing, but making the commitment is well worth your time.

I say this for a couple of reasons. First, you'll become a more educated, well-rounded person. It sounds a bit parental, but you'll gain a lot of general wisdom/knowledge that can benefit

A good investment.

you in the long term. Second, (and more consistent
with the book), it may be important in helping you achieve
your career objectives.

If you're at a pre-interview reception or out to dinner with a
potential employer, it is crucial to be in-the-know. You'll come
off as smart and mature if you have something to talk about
other than the *amazing* party you attended last weekend. This
will be a lot more helpful than you might imagine when you're
standing there awkwardly at a reception attempting to figure out
what you're going to say next to a potential employer. *Seriously*,
if you're standing there for 15 minutes talking to a 52-year-old
corporate recruiter who did not attend your school and is from
a different part of the country or the other side of the globe, you
need something to talk about!

Many recruiters will look almost as heavily at their discussion with you in this informal setting as they will at an interview. In their minds, it's a way to see you in a "real life" setting. It will also create a first impression that will likely stick with them — for better or worse.

Publications like Time, Newsweek, U.S. News and World Report, Businessweek, The Wall Street Journal, and USA Today offer excellent introductory rates for college students. Better yet, much of their content is available online.

Also plan to regularly tune into a news program, or get on the internet to get some perspective on what's going on off campus.

One final point. If you subscribe to a professional publication related to your major (like the Journal of the American Medical Association), you'll probably find it to be difficult reading at first. Stick with it, though. It will get easier. You'll find regular features in a particular publication that seem to relate well to what you're studying. The vocabulary you pick up will be helpful, too. It *will* get easier. I promise.

And, to state the obvious, most major corporations are multinational these days. Many students are intrigued with the idea of working internationally. Many make significant efforts during college, both in and out of the classroom, to position themselves to be strong candidates to companies of this type.

Multinational companies want students who have invested time and effort to become knowledgeable for international roles. How about learning Mandarin in college? Or maybe studying abroad for a semester in a country you'd like to work in some day? A growing number of students are expanding their worlds (and their potential) in these ways. If you want to create specific types of opportunities for yourself, you need to act accordingly.

Expanding your world is a
good investment — of your time
and your money. And, the effort will pay off.

CHAPTER 7
Working Toward Success

If you've made it this far in this book, you probably have a personal goal of "getting a great job after college." I agree 100% with your goal.

Work experience during college can be a major asset toward making this goal a reality. The *right* job experiences can provide

> Work along the way can be a **major plus**.

opportunities to prove that you possess *all* of the **Winning Characteristics** and help you launch a great career. So *if* and *when* you work, work toward success.

In reality, *every* job has *potential* value in this regard. Some inherently offer significantly more opportunities than others. How you approach the job also matters in terms of its potential impact — or lack of it. You need to understand how *any* job you're considering can potentially help you achieve your goal of a great job after college. You *can* get more out of any job than just a paycheck.

I'll categorize college work experiences in three separate groups — jobs (both paid and volunteer ones) during college, summer jobs, and internships. Let's spend a little time on each.

So if and when you work, work toward success.

Jobs During College

When I talk about working during school, I'm not referring to summer vacation or winter break. I'm talking about working while classes are in session. For most college students, working during summer break to help cover college costs is a given. I actually believe that working your tail off at lousy jobs during the summer provides good perspective on life. I'll get into that in the next chapter.

Working *while* school is in session is a fact of life for a growing number of students given the dramatic increases in the cost of college over the past 10 years. If *you* plan to work during the school year, the key question to ask yourself is *WHY*. If you're working to be able to survive — to pay tuition and eat (two fairly noble causes), you obviously need to do so. However, other students work to have extra spending money for pizza, clothes, or weekend fun (which can also be argued to be noble causes). The two are very different.

If you're working because you simply must work to make the economics of college viable, the decision is rather simple — do it. I say this for two reasons. First, you have no choice. It is probably the only way you're going to get through college and it will certainly be a character builder. Second, there is something quite compelling to a recruiter about students who want so badly to get an education that they put forth the **Effort** necessary (and were **Organized** enough) to successfully take on the challenge of working full-time as a student. It's the "American Dream" happening on a personal level. It's impressive and will get a recruiter's attention.

If you do need to work, make every attempt to work in a job that's a step in the direction of your future career. It will give you a look at what you might actually be doing after you graduate *and* will help convince your potential future employer (and you) that you have some talent in and enjoy this field in a non-academic, "real world" setting. If you want to be a pediatric nurse, it will be more helpful for you to work at a day care center than to pull weeds for a landscaping company.

If you don't really *need* to work to pay for school, I would recommend doing so *only* if it results in significant resume building. *Flipping burgers to be able to afford a better brand of beer and a few extra pizzas is a really, Really, REALLY bad idea. (Am I making my point?)* The time you spend in this job probably will do you very little good at interview time. In fact, it could put you at a

significant disadvantage as you'll be competing against students who were doing something more productive with their time.

"Temporary poverty" in college is a lot better than over-commitment to a frivolous endeavor that will get you little or no points on interview day. Besides, you can buy the clothes you want, go out every night, and overdose on pizza *AFTER* you land your dream job. Life doesn't end after college.

It's important to mention that in almost *any* job, paid or volunteer, you can find ways to build the **Winning Characteristics** if you are focused on doing so. You need to proactively *think* about how you'll do that. It may not be immediately obvious and will *NOT* happen unless you make the effort to make it happen.

However, you'll be working on a team, can show creativity, and show you are a hard worker, etc., if you really look for ways to do so. How are you showing leadership by making your company/service organization different or better in your role? Review the **Winning Characteristics** after you get your job and think hard about how you can build them and prove that you now own them via the job. Make sense?

You can get benefit from *any* job if you approach it in the right manner.

One type of work that can be a *very* effective use of your time (and be a lot of fun) is starting your own business. Whether it is a company designing and selling novelty T-shirts and boxer shorts, creating an internet-based business, painting houses, or making and selling flower arrangements, starting your own business is a great way to exhibit the **Winning Characteristics**. If you show that you have what it takes to actually start and run some type of entity, you'll be very popular at interview time.

Let me explain how starting your own business can help you show you possess these characteristics. While he was a sophomore at Harvard, the Co-founder of Making It Count Brad Baker, identified an opportunity in the Boston market and decided to start a T-shirt company to make a few extra bucks.

Among other things, he had to:

- Develop the designs
- Research the production process
- Contract with a manufacturer
- Figure out who would buy these shirts
- Decide what price he could sell them for
- Determine where he could legally sell them
- Identify who would sell them and how much to pay them

He also needed to figure out how to pay for his upfront printing costs. He undoubtedly ran across a number of other barriers and needed to find a way to effectively work through them.

The fact that he took all of these steps to establish the business, made intelligent decisions along the way, and brought the shirts to market — that's a *BIG TIME* accomplishment for a college student! In the endeavor, he demonstrated that he had *each* of the seven **Winning Characteristics**. The fact that he actually made a few bucks in the process was icing on the cake.

A former student of mine named Adam started a prepaid cab company on campus. Parents could pre-purchase cab rides for their students, which were of great benefit after students had spent the evening "uptown." No driving or walking home late at night. Parents liked that. To get the business started, he needed to find drivers with cars. He needed to insure them. He needed to market the service to parents, deal with driver scheduling, car dispatch, etc. It was a real company. He made a lot of money with the business and landed a tremendous job after college because, with all he had done in starting and running the company, he was the poster-child for the **Winning Characteristics**.

I also have neighbors who are college students who started a landscaping business. There is definitely nothing wrong with this approach either! They thought that doing so was a much better way to make a buck to pay for college than wearing *fashionable* uniforms working at a grocery store or fast food restaurant.
I agree. If you do start a business like this, I would strongly suggest you "formalize it." Name it. Create a simple logo and website. Create marketing materials — even if your marketing is just a simple one-page word document that you distribute door-to-door. Create a budget and track your financial performance at the end of each month. Hire employees if you can. All these things transform trimming shrubs into founding a company. Frankly, these efforts will also help get you more shrubs to trim as your marketing should help generate new customers for you. Now you'll have a *growing* business to talk about on interview day! How great is *that*?

So if you're going to work during school, get more out of it than a paycheck. Work toward success.

Summer Jobs

Summer jobs are a way of life for most college students. The money earned in three months of intense work helps to support you for the other nine.

The money earned is definitely an important benefit of these efforts. The job may also offer you a type of incentive you may not have considered. The memory of working 12-hour shifts in 95-degree heat, stacking paper at the end of a dirty printing press for minimum wage, is great incentive to study hard when you're back at school.

Trust me, I've done it. And, if you don't make good decisions while in college, you may be getting an early preview of your future job. Not a pretty thought.

Summer job or a preview of your career?

You'll have *opportunities* to develop and provide concrete examples of the **Winning Characteristics** even with the most unlikely summer job. In three months of work, you'll certainly have some new ideas and thoughts that are a step forward for the organization — if you are focused on building these skills. Without focus, it probably won't happen.

If you work the same summer job for several years, you'll have an even greater opportunity to make an impact. If nothing else, you can certainly exhibit that you're a disciplined, hard worker who will put forth great **Effort** to succeed. And, you can get a strong reference for your future resume from your boss if you do good work (and ask for one).

By the way, every employer is looking for cost-savings opportunities. Many even financially reward employees who can come up with them. Challenge yourself to develop a less expensive way to do what you're doing and present it to your management. Even if they don't pursue it, the fact that you exhibited that type of **Entrepreneurship** can be good ammunition on interview day.

If you can get a job related to your planned career field, it is definitely an added bonus. You'll learn a great deal about what the field is like in the "real world" as opposed to in the classroom. The two can be very, very different. The ultimate chance to do this is an internship.

Even the worst summer job
will provide opportunities to build
the Winning Characteristics.

Internships

I'll be direct here — get one. Better yet, get two... or three. Really! Internships are critical opportunities — almost *mandatory* to a successful job search. You should do anything and everything possible (within the law) to get at least two. In most fields, including business, one isn't always enough any more.

An internship offers you a priceless "test-drive" of your chosen field, and you may even get paid to do it. It's a chance to see what your career field would be like on a day-to-day basis before doing it after you graduate. On a personal note, I completely changed my career direction based on an internship. I *thought* I knew what I wanted to do. I liked the subject in the classroom, but really disliked it in the work setting. My miserable three-month internship was valuable to me — just not in the way I had expected!

Internships give you meaningful "real world" experience that you will carry back to the classroom and into your next job. They may also take some of the fear out of the thought of entering the "real world" that many students experience.

When you interview for the job you want after graduation, internships are critical. They will give you meaty, meaningful discussion topics for the interview itself. You'll have relevant experience "in the field" — always a plus. You'll have your former boss as a reference on your resume — another winner. And, the fact that you *pursued* an internship shows you put forth **Effort** to succeed.

An internship could also be an entrée into the company with which you interned. Many companies now have internship programs to get a closer look at students they think they might like to hire for full-time, permanent positions.

Many major corporations now make a *majority* of their new hires of college graduates from their past interns. It's very logical from their point of view as they get a three-month look at a candidate before having to really make a commitment to him or her. After seeing three or four months of your performance, the employer can make a much more informed hiring decision about you for a permanent job than they could from just interviewing you. And, most interns do meaningful work for firms — so not only do they get a good look at you, they get a good bit of quality work at a very reasonable cost to them.

Even if the internship is not the first step to a full-time job opportunity in a given company, a letter of recommendation from your internship boss can be a strong vote of confidence in the eyes of any recruiter. If you do utilize a letter of recommendation, you need to be ready to answer the question of why you are not going to work after graduation for this highly impressed manager. This is not necessarily a problem. You just need to know the question is coming.

As mentioned before, many students today will have two internships. An internship (typically with a smaller company) between your sophomore and junior years in addition to an internship between junior and senior years is now more common in some fields. It can be a major advantage for business majors to have more than one internship experience under their belts before applying for jobs.

Also, consider the possibility of having an internship *during* the school year through a school office or department. That way if you absolutely need to focus on making money during the summer and need to take a non-career oriented position to maximize your earnings, you can still gain valuable internship experience while building strong relationships with academic leaders.

So… internships are *really* required… but, how do you get them?

There are several ways to get an internship. The first is through the school's formal channels, like the career planning and placement office or via the school's Department Office for your major. Pursue these, but know in advance there will be many applicants competing for a limited number of jobs.

You'll also want to be aggressive about seeking out internships on your own. Utilize online resources like Monster.com, etc. There are literally thousands of internships advertised online every day. Read all Internet postings carefully. Many will be legitimate. Others will not be. When you're looking online and dealing with companies you haven't previously heard of, be skeptical and ask a lot of questions to understand the company and what specifically you'll be doing in the job. If it's an insurance firm that really just wants you to sell insurance to your family and friends, it may not be what you're looking for. On the other hand, you may find a tremendous opportunity with a growing company that doesn't yet have a formal recruiting relationship with your college.

You can also send out resumes to local companies. Call the companies and get the names of their personnel directors and department heads. You *may* also find those names online on the companies' websites. Always follow up with a phone call after sending out your resume and cover letter (even though you may find this a bit uncomfortable), attempting to set up a meeting to at least talk about what the options may be. Offer to take key contacts to lunch. As busy as they may be, they do eat lunch.

You can offer to pay and not be taken up on it in most cases. They have expense accounts and know you don't so will often pick up the tab.

If you meet with potential employers and they are impressed, if they can't hire you, they may recommend you to friends in the business. They may also *create* an internship if their company is doing well and they think you are a good potential future full-time hire. Don't be shy about asking for referrals to other potential employers if they can't offer you an opportunity but seem to like you. If you don't get out of your comfort zone and really be aggressive here (in a polite way, of course), you're not likely to have much success.

Don't overlook small companies. They may be even more interested than large ones. They may truly need some of your expertise and not be able to afford to hire someone full-time to perform that function. Their company name may not look quite as good as Google on your resume, but you'll probably have as meaningful a learning experience as you'd get at a big company. You may actually get a lot more "real work" to do than in a big company because the small firm simply doesn't have the resources to have a full-time employee do the work. And, your relationship with your supervisor could be closer in a smaller organization as the atmosphere may be a bit more casual.

Finally, this setting may give you a feel for some of the pros and cons of ultimately going to work for a small company versus a big one.

Remember, there's no formal definition of an internship. Even if a company has never hired an intern, you can help them create an internship program. If you're doing full-time work in your field of study and gaining experience while helping an organization achieve its business goals, it's an internship! This is particularly true between your sophomore and junior years. Many "big name" firms aren't going to give you an internship after your second year of college, but when the big name firms interview you when you're a junior for an internship opportunity *next* summer, *any* internship experience you have to talk about during the interview is a plus.

If you don't know what companies are in your town, utilize the local Chamber of Commerce as a resource. Try to get an appointment with the executive director and let her know how hard you are willing to work and how little you need to be paid. You may ask her to let her Chamber Board of Directors know of your interest. A follow-up letter or e-mail from you after the meeting will make this more likely to happen. An e-mail is actually better as she can forward it to her board members quickly and easily. You will also want to mention that you'd like to work in this area long term. She'll like that — and so will her board.

You can also look online to find out which companies are the largest employers in the area. Just Google your city name and "largest companies" and you'll get a ranked list based on their number of employees. It's a great starting point in terms of where to look.

Use contacts (like your parents, your neighbors, etc.) to get your foot in the door. Look to the parents of your college friends who may work in related fields. Yes, I know this may be a bit awkward, but it will be *MUCH* less awkward than trying to get a full-time job as a senior with *no* internships. You'll be amazed how willing people will be to help if you approach them in a respectful, sincere way and they take away the perception that you're a dedicated student who's willing to work to get the job done.

With some **Effort**, you'll find people who will give you a chance. Some of your favorite professors may also be able to help. Many have tremendous contacts (past students) at companies that are employers of people from your major and school. If you've impressed the professor with your work in his class, he may go to bat for you.

Offer to work for a low wage or even free if you can afford it! Some of the best internships available are unpaid positions. And, a small company that would love the help but doesn't have the budget for it will be *much* more likely to give you the opportunity if it doesn't cost any money.

You may have to wait tables at night to pay your bills if you take an unpaid internship, but better now than after college when you'll be trying to pay off student loans!

Just get the experience. It will pay off for you in the long run.

CHAPTER 8
Putting It All Together

Wow! This sure sounds complicated. You'll need to do a million different things, including picking the right major, learning how to study in a whole new way, picking professors well, getting into their heads, learning where and how to study, taking tests well, playing organized sports, running an organization, and getting an internship — or two. It's overwhelming!

Actually, it's not all that bad. You can have fun, make some friends for life, and land the job you want. It all comes down to having a good plan and seeing the plan through.

It all comes down to having a **good plan**.

The next five sections and the appendix will help simplify what "getting the job done" will mean

You can rise above it and succeed.

for you personally. The sections will also share a semester-by-semester schedule for you to use as a reference guide. It all comes down to having a good plan and seeing the plan through, right?

Every piece of advice in this book is not meant to be followed literally. That said, the items in the schedule and the recommended timing for them will be on-target for most students in most majors at most schools.

The upcoming sections will also give you the opportunity to set some personal goals for yourself. Take the time and make the commitment to complete the goal-setting exercise.

And finally, you'll get some tips on how long your college experience should last.

Take them to heart.

Setting goals is the first step
on the road to success.

How Long It Should Take

Let me start by saying that your parents did not pay me to write this chapter. I just happen to have strong feelings on this subject.

Four years.
Not five years.
Not six years.
And certainly not seven.

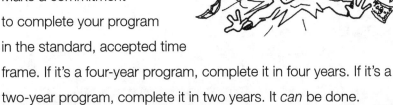

Make a commitment
to complete your program
in the standard, accepted time
frame. If it's a four-year program, complete it in four years. If it's a two-year program, complete it in two years. It *can* be done.

Really.

If nothing else, think about the cost of the "extra" year. First, there's the tuition. Then there's the room and board. Now let's talk about what I'll call the "opportunity loss."

If you had graduated on time, you would have been making, not spending, money during that extra year. So, take the actual tuition and room and board costs of the fifth year and add on the $40,000 job "opportunity" you gave up by not being out in the "real world" earning it. The fifth year is *VERY* expensive if you combine your educational costs *and* the earnings you gave up because you were in school.

Your "five-year degree" will be no more valuable to you than if you get it in four years. On the five-year "plan" (or three-year "plan" at a community college), it will just cost a lot more for the same diploma.

When you think about it that way, the extra year becomes a little more expensive and a little less attractive, doesn't it?

The other cost associated with the extra year is what I call the "credibility cost." It is the immediate negative reaction on the part of a recruiter that you were not able to complete your academic program on time. If it's a four-year program, they want to know you completed it in four years — or know *WHY NOT?* In a fast-paced world with lots of deadlines, a five-year experience does not give you immediate credibility with recruiters.

As with anything else, there are exceptions to this rule. If you make a significant change in your major during your junior or senior year, take a six-to-nine month internship, have failing health, financial problems, etc., it may be perfectly legitimate to extend your college experience for another year. And, some programs are designed to be five years or longer in duration and may include a semester abroad to study European architecture or history. These situations can be easily explained and should not pose a major problem. In fact, true five-year programs that include study abroad or meaningful work experience can be seen as a tremendous asset.

You may be able to quickly justify a fifth year to a recruiter and have a very successful interview. An unnecessary extra year is just not a great place to start an interview.

If it's a standard four-year program, plan on completing it in four years.

A Simplified Look
at What It Takes

You're more than 200 pages into the book. Now I'll boil everything I've talked about into just a few pages to leave you thinking about how *YOU* will build *YOUR* future.

If you're going to college to get a great job or change the world, you need to understand what a recruiter will be looking for when you get out. They're looking for the **Winning Characteristics**:

1. **Communication skills:** Being able to make your point in writing and verbally *and* being able to really *listen* to and comprehend the points made by others.

2. **Organizational skills:** Being able to prioritize and to get and stay on top of multiple activities.

3. **Leadership:** The ability to move a team, to make good things happen.

4. Logic: Good old-fashioned smarts and problem-solving skills, from analytical ability to creativity.

5. Effort: A very strong desire to succeed, having the will to win and taking the actions necessary to make things happen.

6. Group skills: Being a part of a team with an ability to successfully lead and follow *and* knowing when a situation calls for leadership or for being a follower.

7. Entrepreneurship: Being a person with new ideas and having the ability to make them realities.

8. Ethics: Being a trustworthy, honest person of character.

To launch your career, you'll need concrete examples to prove that you have these characteristics. You'll do this in three ways: 1) with strong grades, 2) an impressive record in extracurricular activities (including purposeful volunteer service), and 3) meaningful internship/work experiences.

From an academic standpoint, a 3.0 cumulative GPA gets you in the game for a good job, a 3.5 average puts you in the driver's seat for a great job. But don't expect these numbers to come easily.

You'll need to make some very good decisions to achieve them. College isn't easy. It's not supposed to be.

In terms of extracurriculars, it's the quality, not the quantity, that will make the difference. *Meaningful* efforts and contributions will help prove you have the desired **Winning Characteristics**. A meaningless laundry list of clubs and activities is all but worthless.

Work experience can be a tremendous asset. Internships, in particular, are excellent opportunities to build and exhibit the **Winning Characteristics**. Choose all of your work and volunteer experiences wisely to make sure you're working toward success.

With good time management, you can accomplish these

objectives and still have the time of your life during your college career.

So there it is — in just a few pages — your road map to success in college. Think about it, focus on it, and make it happen for you.

It's not brain surgery.
It's just understanding the keys to success
and making them a part of your personal
college and career game plan.

Semester-by-Semester Guide

You can't wake up the second semester of your senior year and decide you're going to follow the principles in this book. It's too late. *The party is over.*

An analogy used by the noted author and speaker Stephen Covey is the "Law of the Harvest." The same principle holds true here. Attempting to accomplish a lot of the principles and objectives spelled out in this book at the very end of your college career would be similar to a farmer planting his corn in August and expecting a good crop in October. He can pull all nighters, fertilizing and watering the crops, giving it 100% to try to catch up. It won't work. Even though you're probably not a farmer, I'll bet you're not surprised that the farmer's catch-up plan failed miserably. It's common sense.

Okay then, because success in college is a building process, how can you expect to do well unless you make the effort early and consistently throughout your years there? *You can't. I promise you. It just won't work!*

Okay, enough with the sermons. Here's the schedule. It's just a guideline, but it will provide you with some important insight. I've created it based on a semester schedule. If you're on quarters, you'll need to make some minor adjustments, but the principles still apply.

Freshman Year - Semester 1
First and foremost, get your feet planted firmly on the ground. This is your opportunity to get adjusted. Your first year is *NOT* a transition year. It's the foundation for your future.

Don't be fooled into thinking you can fall behind and catch up later. You can't. About one out of eight students never successfully completes the first semester.

Your goal here is *not* to see how many nights in a row you can party. You will find many people who will tell you it is. Get to

know them while you can. They won't be there next semester.
Your goal is to make the Dean's List (typically requires a 3.5
GPA). Freshmen *DO* make the Dean's List. You can too!
Look for a couple of organizations to join. Get active in
those groups immediately. Get to know the leadership of the
organizations and look for ways to contribute.

Find out when fraternity and sorority membership drives (called
rush) are held. They will be held either once or twice a year. If
you're interested in potentially joining, you won't want to miss
the dates.

Other organizations you might want to pursue may be related
to your major or a hobby/interest you have. Campus bulletin
boards, campus websites, and the student newspapers are
also excellent ways to learn about extracurricular opportunities.
Some schools have activity fairs to showcase opportunities. If
your school has these, *go to them!*

And, if I haven't mentioned it lately, college is the big leagues. Study hard or you're going to get buried.

Freshman Year - Semester 2

Okay, you survived. Good for you. Now, where to go from here? If your grades aren't what they need to be, look hard at 1) the quality and quantity of effort you've *really* given, 2) your time management, and 3) the quality of your study techniques. Don't give up. You can do it.

Go deeper in terms of your involvement on campus. As I mentioned, if you're not already a member of at least two organizations, just reading the bulletin boards and school paper will make you aware of many opportunities. Remember, you'll be running for office in these groups next year. People will need to know who you are (and know you're a quality individual) to vote for you!

Make sure you have visited your school's career planning and placement office. Go now and become a regular there. You'll be looking to get career-related work experience in the *very* near future. Make sure they know you and think of you *FIRST* when opportunities arise.

And remember, if you're not already there, you need to get your grades up to or above 3.0, or better yet, 3.5.

Sophomore Year - Semester 1

You're no longer a rookie. You're now a seasoned veteran. You'll be taking more classes related to your major and digging into some more specialized subject matter.

Take on responsibility in the organizations you've joined. You're not going to get a top position in these groups until you have proven yourself capable in lesser ones. Run for minor offices and offer to run committees. Do whatever is necessary to establish credibility within these organizations.

What are you doing next summer? If you want to have two internships during college (which is a good idea), your first one will be next summer! Go to the career planning and placement office and see what the opportunities are for you to get some career-related work experience next summer. I know you think it's too early to do this. It's not. You've got to trust me on this one and start thinking about internships.

Sophomore Year - Semester 2

You ought to be hitting your stride. You now understand how to get the grades you'll need and should be making the personal commitment to reach your targeted GPA.

If you're not making some progress with extracurricular activities, *NOW* is the time to start. If you wait, you'll be too late. If you're struggling to make progress in larger organizations, look at smaller clubs as a way to make an impact.

If you're thinking about starting up a business or any type of organization, it's not too early to write your business plan and launch it. What are you waiting for? At the end of this semester, you're halfway done!

While most of your major out-of-classroom achievements are probably still ahead of you, you ought to have your plans to achieve them well mapped out.

Have you finalized your employment plans for the summer yet? If not, it's time. Try to find a job that will give you any kind of experience related to your desired career field.

Junior Year - Semester 1

You're still tracking well academically (if not, *MEMORIZE* chapter 5).

You're pursuing leadership positions in organizations on and off campus. You're aggressively working to develop the **Winning Characteristics**. You'll have some failures along the way, some elections you don't win and some goals you don't achieve. But, believe it or not, *everybody* fails. It's an important part of the learning process. *THIS* is your year for extracurricular accomplishments. Don't let this critical year slip away without making an impact!

By the way, what are you doing to get an internship? Or, better yet, are you working on landing your second internship?

Junior Year - Semester 2

If you haven't landed your internship for this summer, push harder toward this goal. Get creative. Go back and read the section on internships. Get to work. Use your contacts. And, get an internship!

Keep working away on projects outside the classroom. How are you personally making your organization *different* and *better*?

This is what you'll talk about in your interviews!

Most of the classes you're taking are in your major. Remember, you want your average in your major to be higher than your overall average.

In some ways, this is your last semester. If you're tracking as you should be, you'll have secured a full-time job during the first semester of your senior year.

Push hard this semester!

As a final thought, you'll also want to really hone your ever-improving resume this semester. If it's not what you want it to be, look at what *meaningful* things you can do over the next six months to make it stronger.

Senior Year - Semester 1

It's time to start your job search in a *MAJOR* way. Your resume should be well-polished and you should start interviewing for jobs. It is important that you understand that many of the best employers will make the majority of their offers during the first semester in an attempt to garner the most talented students available. Most of these offers will require a yes/no decision from you within 60 days (or less), so be prepared to interview broadly so you understand your options before having to make a decision.

You're in the home stretch in all aspects of your college experience. Keep your grades up and keep pushing in terms of your extracurricular activities. If you don't make some things happen now, you're probably not going to! If you don't land the job you want early in the recruiting process, your accomplishments this semester may set you apart in your final semester as you continue to interview.

Senior Year - Semester 2

Be confident. Be aggressive. Go get that job you want (if you haven't already).

Interview as much as you can. Work closely with your school's career planning and placement office to make sure your resume is well written. This will greatly affect how heavily you are recruited. Many of these offices will conduct practice interviews with you and/or videotape you in a practice interview.

Personally contact organizations you would like to work for that are not visiting your school. I've seen that approach pay off many times.

Look at online job search resources. Don't be limited by your college's career center and what it can offer you. Also, see what you can find on your own! Remember the value of networking.

Rather than write another eight sections on how to interview, I will simply tell you to utilize all the resources available through your career placement office. Be honest, be confident, and sell yourself thoroughly (you've only got one chance to set yourself apart). Make sure you have done some research on the interviewing companies/organizations. If you were a recruiter, you wouldn't hire someone who says, "I don't know what your organization does, but I do know I want to work there. I hear it's a great place to work?" Make sure the recruiter knows that you are serious candidate who really wants to work for his or her company.

You've laid the proper foundation by following the principles in this book so *YOU SHOULD BE IN EXCELLENT SHAPE.*

Starting Right Now

Let's talk a bit more about the here and now.

With your 10-year plan in mind and with all of the new "wisdom" you now possess, take some time and write down your goals for the next 12 months.

Don't wait or you may never do it. *Do it NOW!*

Look at what you will accomplish in terms of academics, involvement in extracurriculars, and other personal or work goals. Your goals don't need to be earth shattering. They just have to be realistic, and preferably accomplishments you can measure (to know if you achieved them or not). And please, don't forget the **Winning Characteristics**.

You can write your goals right here in the book or in a separate location. Invest a little time in doing this and then post and track your results.

A couple of hints. Be realistic. Save the thoughts of rock and roll fame for another day.

Your targets don't all have to be dramatic achievements. Just make sure they are meaningful, both in the absolute and to you personally. Look at things you have a reasonable shot at accomplishing, but do dream *BIG*.

Here are a few examples of goals:

Academic

    1. Achieve a _____ GPA.

    2. Miss no more than _____ classes in a semester.

    3. Study _____ hours a day.

    4. Study at least _____ hours for each exam.

Extracurricular

    1. Find and join two organizations related to my major or areas of interest. Go to meetings and volunteer to help.

    2. Get on at least two committees and do something to help in a meaningful way.

3. Commit at least two hours a week to a community service effort and work to help that organization meet its goals.

Work

1. Consistently look for ways to utilize my job to build the **Winning Characteristics**. Find measurable ways I helped improve the organization.
2. Present at least one new idea a month to my boss on how I can help improve the company.

Personal/General

1. Get up by 8 a.m. every day, Monday through Friday.
2. Spend 60 minutes a week keeping up with current events in my field (and the world, in general).

Take on the pain. Spend the time. Set some goals related to the **Winning Characteristics**.

Set goals **today** then make them a reality.

12 Month Goals/Worksheet

Academic

1. _____
2. _____
3. _____
4. _____
5. _____

Extracurricular Activities

1. _____
2. _____
3. _____
4. _____
5. _____

Work/Personal

1. _____
2. _____
3. _____
4. _____
5. _____

Set your goals!
Cut along dotted line and post where
you can see them *EVERY DAY*.

CLOSING THOUGHTS

Well, there it is — my "definitive" guide on how to approach college to set yourself up to achieve your future dreams. While every student is different and every school is different, follow this approach and, in the long run, you'll be well ahead of the pack. It works. I'm living proof of it. Letters and personal testimonials from students who read and followed the path offered in the original edition of "Making College Count" prove this guide can work for you too!

This is *not* an easy approach. Winning approaches rarely are. But, if my future depended on my success in college (as yours does to a large extent), I would follow a proven approach (like this one) rather than fumbling through without a game plan and hoping for the best.

I've hit you with a tremendous amount of material. There's no way you could have absorbed all of it. Make a personal commitment to read the book again in six months. Really! I'm serious. How long will it take? Three hours? Three-and-a-half? It's a great investment of time.

After six months in college, you'll read it at a different level and get some additional benefit from it. To stay on track, you may even want to take notes-notes as you read next time around and review them every six months. It won't take long and will save you time when you want to refer to the book at the beginning of your sophomore and junior years.

Set goals. Put them somewhere where you'll see them and then make them a reality. Tracking your progress will reinforce that you're moving in the right direction as you meet individual goals on your list, and it will keep you focused on what's important to you in a fast-paced environment loaded with distractions.

College really is one of the best times in your life. It certainly was for me and should be for you. Just make sure that while you're having all that fun, you're setting yourself up to have the best and most rewarding career possible for the many decades that follow.

Knock 'em dead.

APPENDIX
Your Personal Score Sheets

The following sheets will help you track your progress throughout college by helping you objectively determine if you are "on track" to success. They'll also be a big help when it comes time to put together your resume and/or applications to graduate school.

Freshman Year

Class	Professor	Grade
_____	_____	_____
_____	_____	_____
_____	_____	_____
_____	_____	_____
_____	_____	_____
_____	_____	_____
_____	_____	_____
_____	_____	_____
_____	_____	_____

Year End GPA: _____

GPA in major (if you have selected a major): _____

Notable Successes: Extracurricular/Community Service

_____

_____

Notable Successes: Work

_____

_____

Possible References

_____

_____

Visited the career planning and placement office? YES or NO

Sophomore Year

Class	Professor	Grade
_____	_____	_____
_____	_____	_____
_____	_____	_____
_____	_____	_____
_____	_____	_____
_____	_____	_____
_____	_____	_____
_____	_____	_____
_____	_____	_____

Year End GPA: _____

GPA in major (if you have selected a major): _____

Notable Successes: Extracurricular/Community Service

_____

_____

Notable Successes: Work/Internship

_____

_____

Possible References

_____

_____

Visited the career planning and placement office? YES or NO

Junior Year

Class	Professor	Grade
_____	_____	_____
_____	_____	_____
_____	_____	_____
_____	_____	_____
_____	_____	_____
_____	_____	_____
_____	_____	_____
_____	_____	_____
_____	_____	_____

Year End GPA: _____

GPA in major: _____

Notable Successes: Extracurricular/Community Service

_____

_____

Notable Successes: Work/Internship

_____

_____

Possible References

_____

_____

Visited the career planning and placement office? YES or NO

Senior Year

Class	Professor	Grade
_____	_____	_____
_____	_____	_____
_____	_____	_____
_____	_____	_____
_____	_____	_____
_____	_____	_____
_____	_____	_____
_____	_____	_____
_____	_____	_____

Year End GPA: _____

GPA in major: _____

Notable Successes: Extracurricular/Community Service

_____

_____

Notable Successes: Work/Internship

_____

_____

References

_____

_____

"*Lived*" at the career planning and placement office? YES or NO

FEEDBACK
Reaction to the *Original* Making College Count

"Insightful keys to success in college — a practical how-to for ANY student. Should be packed in every freshman's duffel bag."

—D. Samuel Neill
Chairman, University of North Carolina Board of Governors

"A real eye-opener. I'm much better prepared having read this very informative and enjoyable book."

—Andrea Tweeten
Freshman, Princeton University

"The must-use, practical guide for today's college student. Don't just buy it — use it — and begin down the path of success."

—Donn Davis
Senior Vice President, AOL

"A long needed and easily understood guide for effectively putting higher education to work. One of the best I've seen in my 44 years in the college services field."

—Maurice Mayberry
Career Resource Center Director Emeritus, University of Florida

"It presents college-bound students with the secrets to success. It should be required reading for all incoming first-year college students."

—Dr. Roberta Sue Alexander
Director, First Year Experience Program, University of Dayton

"In 23 years of recruiting, I have learned that the characteristics defined by O'Brien are key to laying the groundwork for a productive and fulfilling career in business, in the professions, even in the arts."

—Heath W. Smith
Executive Recruiter

"'Making College Count' is invaluable preparation for future success. There's nothing else like it."

—Larry Zigerelli
Vice President/Country Manager, Procter & Gamble

"'Making College Count' draws an on-the-money connection between college and career… and gives practical, no-nonsense advice on how to make the connection work."

—James M. Holec, Jr.
Management Consulting Partner, PricewaterhouseCoopers

"'Making College Count' deserves a place on the shelves of every high school library and should be required reading for every graduating senior. Blessedly more of a conversation than a lecture, it is part reality-check and part self-help manual for those looking to make the most of their college years."

—Dianne Young
Senior Writer, Southern Living

"An easy guide that can, in an hour or two, help students avoid wasting years of their life or wasting opportunities of a lifetime."

—Randy Scott
Vice President Marketing, Nine West Group, Inc.

"A book like this is long overdue. I'm sorry it did not exist when I went to college. It's TERRIFIC."

—Michael Grossman
President, Rim Pacific Imports

"It is indeed encouraging to read something that can be of GREAT assistance to our youth who are willing to make the commitment. 'Making College Count' is an excellent piece of work and should be a must-read for all who are considering a college education."

—J.B. "Jack" Curcio
Retired-President, Chairman, Mack Trucks, Inc.

"As president of a successful, entrepreneurial company as well as a father with two children in college, I feel this book is a must-read for college freshmen. All the principles that helped jump-start my career are here and they're presented in a way that appeals to students. Both my son and daughter enjoyed the book and felt it was a tremendous asset."

—Roger Kimps
President & CEO, Graphic Management Corporation

"The book offers no easy road to success; however, it will help future college students avoid the pitfalls many students stumble into. O'Brien has explained in a very readable form practices and approaches that worked well for him, and should work well for all students entering college today."

—Dr. David Sink
President, Blue Ridge Community College

"Having interviewed and recruited hundreds of individuals during my career, I feel confident saying the principles of this book are right on target. I would strongly recommend it for students serious about success in college and, more importantly, after graduation."

—Larry Baker
Sr. Vice President Administration, Wausau Papers

"Very insightful. Timeless wisdom combined with some very innovative thoughts. All in a very student-friendly format."

—Carlos Rodriquez
Vice President Operations, Vincam
Harvard Business School Graduate

"No matter which career path you plan to pursue, this book will help get you to wherever you want to go."

—Tom Southworth
Counselor, Wausau East High School

"I particularly liked the way it linked school to the job market and the concept of making your time count. It is a good life lesson… work hard and have fun too! The Winning Characteristics are right on the mark and are what employers are looking for."

—Lori Glander
Training & Development Specialist, MILSCO Manufacturing Corporation

"All the things you want your children to know and understand, but must hear from another person. I have made it a must-read for our six children. It provides extremely valuable information that can be as important as the diploma itself."

—Tom Fazio
World's Leading Golf Course Architect

"'Making College Count' should be required reading for every high school student! Reading the book is like having a one-on-one conversation with a mentor who really knows what lies ahead for a student, and also knows how a student can get a jump-start in his/her life."

—Duane McKibbin
President/Owner Henderson Oil Co., Inc.
Stanford University Graduate School of Business, MBA

"I have been recruiting senior-level management for corporations since 1983. During this time I have found that out of the thousands of people I have interviewed, approximately 90% of them did not have any idea as to what they should pursue in college. Similarly, the same percentage today are employed in a different profession than the major they pursued in college. This book gives clear focus on positioning yourself to a rewarding career after college. It takes the guesswork out of your career direction. Well done! This book should be a required course in high school."

—Dennis J. Caruso
Managing Partner, Caruso & Associates, Inc.
Executive Search Consultants

"With the significant financial commitment involved in attending college today, a book such as 'Making College Count' offers its readers a game plan that will ultimately protect their college investment."

—Laura Hardy
Southern Regional Campaign Director
Juvenile Diabetes Foundation International

"'Making College Count' is the 'In Search of Excellence' of college preparation books. Well-organized and written in an incredibly easy-to-read style, this book is sure to be a must-read for anyone contemplating a college education."

—Chuck Mitchell
Senior Vice President, The Branigar Organization, Inc.

"Given my extensive involvement in education, I'm very excited about 'Making College Count' and the positive impact it will have on today's students."

—Julie Pyburn
Educational Speaker and Consultant

"The author's insights and advice amount to the keys to success in today's competitive job market. My former students who have been the top targets of recruiters have achieved that lofty status by preparing themselves in the manner so eloquently described by the author. 'Making College Count' is required reading for my own teenagers as they are starting to make their college and career choices."

—Donald G. Norris Ph.D.
Associate Marketing Professor, Miami University
University of California, Berkeley

"Having spent two years with Pat as his college roommate and close friend, I can say that his philosophies and principles are practical and sound! Simply put, his plan works!"

—Joe Williams
Sales Manager, Schlage Lock Company